Television Culture and Women's Lives

University of Pennsylvania Press
Feminist Cultural Studies, the Media, and Political Culture

Mary Ellen Brown and Andrea Press, Editors

Margaret J. Heide. *Television Culture and Women's Lives: thirtysomething and the Contradictions of Gender.* 1995

Television Culture and Women's Lives

thirtysomething and the Contradictions of Gender

Margaret J. Heide

University of Pennsylvania Press

Philadelphia

Printed in the United States of America

Library of Congress Cataloging-in-Publication Data

Heide, Margaret J.
Television cultur and women's lives : thirtysomething and the contradictions of gender / Margaret J. Heide.
p. cm. — (Feminist cultural studies, the media, and political culture)
Includes bibliographical references (p.) and index.
ISBN 0-8122-3253-4 (cloth). — ISBN 0-8122-1534-6 (pbk.)
1. Thirtysomething (Television program) 2. Women in telrvision—United States. 3. Television and women—United States. I. Title. II. Series.
PN 1992.77.T558H45 1995
791.45'72—dc20 94-41723
CIP

To my mother and Bill,
for everything

Contents

Acknowledgments

Writing a book about television and women's lives has turned out to be an emotionally rewarding and challenging process. For the women I interviewed are living through very difficult times, as they try to negotiate between the oftentimes competing roles they are called on to occupy. Television was one arena they drew on to help make sense of these conflicts. Chronicling these efforts was therefore illuminating. I am extraordinarily grateful to all the women who contributed to this book for their interviews and feedback. In the process, they helped me to understand the difficulties I too have found in trying to balance the ever greater claims women have on their time and emotional energy. I am also grateful to the creators of *thirtysomething*, Edward Zwick and Marshall Herskovitz, and all the writers and directors and actors on the show, for crafting a program which was able to respond so effectively to so many individuals' lives. That the solutions they arrived at on the program were not always progressive or transformative does not lessen the impact they were able to have on their viewing audience. This power to affect viewers made it an ideal vehicle for thinking about how television creates a culture which audiences draw on to think about their own lives.

In addition to the viewers and creators of *thirtysomething*, there are a number of people I would like to thank for helping to make this project a reality. This book is based on my dissertation research. My dissertation committee at the Graduate Faculty of the New School for Social Research, including Jeffrey Goldfarb, Andrew Arato, and Ann Snitow, were extremely helpful and encouraging to me throughout all the stages of dissertation writing. Their intelligent and thoughtful criticism helped to strengthen my arguments.

I would also like to thank my editor Patricia Smith of the University of Pennsylvania Press and Dr. Andrea Press at the University of Michigan for their belief in this project and their sustained and insightful feedback on all stages of the manuscript. Anonymous reviewers' comments on the original manuscript were also key to helping reformulate some of my findings. Managing editor Alison Anderson and Doris Braendel also deserve special thanks for their wonderful job of copyediting the manuscript. I am wholly responsible for any errors or omissions that may have occurred.

A number of friends and colleagues lent their support along the way. Carla Freeman from the University of North Carolina at Chapel Hill and Donna Goldstein at the University of Colorado at Boulder provided their considerable insights from their field of cultural anthropology to my study; in addition, Abby Scher, Perry Chang, Amy Siskind, and Susan Pearce from the Graduate Faculty were sharp critics and astute readers of earlier versions of this manuscript. Laura Cates, Aileen Gribbin, and Mei Mei Woo were also extremely supportive friends and commentators. I am also grateful to my colleagues at SUNY/Empire State College, including Rhoda Miller and Douglas Johnstone, who gave me the time and freedom to complete this project.

In addition to friends and colleagues, I would also like to acknowledge my family, including Marjorie and Paul Heide, Wilbur Fried, Lisa Gordon, and Joan Tally, who, together with Svetlana and Semyon Elkind, provided crucial baby-sitting while I was rushing to complete deadlines. This book owes its greatest debt to my life partner and friend, Bill Tally. He has not only served as an editor and intellectual muse, but provided a model for thinking critically.

Finally, my daughter Lila, who was born right after I completed the dissertation, has been an inspiration. Her appropriation of female gender identity at such an early age has served as a sobering note to her mother on just how powerful gender roles can be. I am in debt to her, and to my grandmother Therese Bernhard, for giving me the insight and courage to imagine different lives for women.

Chapter 1

Gender and Generation: The Case of *thirtysomething*

To look at television today is to enter a world that is at once fantastic and eerily familiar. One way television makes claim to the familiar is to draw on existing conflicts in American society, commenting on them in comfortable and well-known forms (Gitlin 1985:12; Taylor 1989:3; Newcomb and Hirsch 1984:63). Television not only is able to draw on social crises and anxieties, it has become one of the primary resources that individuals rely on to help them make sense of the world and of their actions in the world (Jensen 1984:108).

Observing this capacity of network television to serve as a kind of cultural forum that organizes and shapes our understanding of our social selves, I became interested in exploring how television frames ideas about gender and the family for the post-World War II so-called "baby-boom" generation. For this generation is the first in history to have lived not only through a large-scale movement for women's liberation but at the same time through the historically unprecedented entry of great numbers of women into the paid labor force (Silberstein 1992; Gerstel and Gross 1987). These two factors have created a tremendous upheaval in the lives of women, which television in turn tries to represent (Silberstein 1992:ix). Shows from *That Girl* in the 1960s to *The Mary Tyler Moore Show* in the 1970s to *One Day at a Time* in the 1980s have provided public images, for example, of white middle-class women's entry into the labor force.

These images on television, furthermore, are not neutral but often reflect competing interests as to how social life should be organized. A conservative vision of work and family life affirms the traditional division of men and women into separate "spheres," where women primarily occupy the private sphere of the home and men the public sphere of the paid labor force. A more liberal vision, on the other hand, entertains a variety of flexible social arrangements to be negotiated between partners, with both men and women participating fully in home life as well as the paid labor force.[1]

The media feud over out-of-wedlock births that broke out between Dan Quayle and the producers of *Murphy Brown* during the 1992 presidential campaign is just one example of how competing ideologies about women's place in the family and work confront each other on tv screens. In such disparate television formats as celebrity talk shows, the evening news, situation comedies, and dramas the battle over competing visions of gender is waged. Television thus serves as a site of contestation, reflecting contemporary struggles over gender and family (Barrett 1980:112).

One of the most ambitious efforts to represent the family in the last decade is the network television series *thirtysomething*, now in rerun on the Lifetime cable channel. An hour-long dramatic series, *thirtysomething* aired from 1987 to 1991, in the twilight of a decade in which the post-war generations came of age. Set in an area somewhere outside Philadelphia, *thirtysomething* revolves around the personal lives of seven friends in their thirties: Michael Steadman and his wife, Hope, the primary characters; Elliot Weston, Michael's business partner and close friend, and his wife, Nancy; Melissa Steadman, Michael's cousin; Gary Shepherd, Michael's oldest friend; and Ellyn Warren, Hope's oldest friend. Of the main characters, five are married and have children; two are single women. All of them are white, well-educated, middle and upper middle class; all have had or are currently pursuing careers.

The plots of *thirtysomething* usually center on personal crises or events that the characters are facing in their work or family life, and the main "action" consists of discussions between the characters about these events. This primary focus on the characters' work and family lives is in keeping with what the producers, Edward Zwick and Marshall Herskovitz, wanted to explore in their effort to capture the "small moments" of people's lives as a means of creating a bond between the characters and the viewing audience.[2]

In terms of the problem of gender, some of the day-to-day or "real life" conflicts the married female characters Hope and Nancy go through revolve around wanting to go back into the paid labor force versus wanting to stay home with their children full time; wanting to be taken seriously as autonomous individuals versus wanting to be immersed in the mothering role; wanting equality with their mates versus wanting to be "taken care of"; and more generally, trying to communicate and establish sexual intimacy with their spouses, relating to their single women friends, and dealing with the conflicting burdens of home, family, and their desire to find meaningful outside employment.

The single women characters Melissa Steadman and Ellyn Warren, for their part, experience conflicts over pursuing their careers while at the same time finding men and getting married; over dealing with the social pressure of *not* being married; over wanting to have freedom versus wanting to be in a relationship; and, finally, over wanting to have children before their biological clock runs out or coming to terms with their recognition that they do not want children. The men on the show also experience a variety of conflicts relating to what kind of role they should play in their marriage, family, and work lives, and the show deals with men's ambivalent feelings toward fulfilling traditional roles as well (Hanke 1990). Through exploring these conflicts, the makers of *thirtysomething* hoped to reach a large and affluent, primarily white audience who were themselves grappling with a whole new set of confusing and bewildering choices as to how to negotiate their work and family lives (O'Connor 1989:C20). A key premise behind the great bulk of episodes is that the characters' life choices involve mutually exclusive goals that their parents did not have to face. At the root of this lies a changing sexual division of labor: being a good mother and wife might now conflict with being a successful professional; being a good provider economically might now be insufficient to be counted as a good husband and father (Zwick and Herskovitz 1991:3).

While confronting many of the same problems that their parents faced, then, this new generation also find themselves in the position of having to choose what kind of life and what gender roles they want to adopt. Far from being a liberating experience, this ability to choose is experienced as a psychic and emotional burden attended by a great deal of pain and confusion. Ultimately, Zwick and Herskovitz perceive their stories as revealing an important truth about the moral and political choices facing their generation, choices that involve fundamental conflicts over the self-conscious creation of social and gender identities. This is the source of the pervasive sense of anxiety, self-doubt, and complaint that the main characters, despite their affluence, typically feel.

As it turns out, this emphasis on capturing the "stuff of real life" by exploring contemporary gender conflicts struck a deep chord not only in the viewing audience it was targeted toward, the baby boomers, but in the larger culture as well. *Thirtysomething* was a critical and commercial success, being nominated for and winning numerous Emmy awards including, in its first broadcast year, "Outstanding Dramatic Series." The program attracted an enormous amount of attention from the mainstream media as well as from the television industry and entertainment press. Much of this attention centered on its uncanny ability to reach the baby-boom generation to which it was marketed.[3] One com-

audiences they were targeted to.[4] From this original parry toward the "new generation," programs such as *Baby Boom, Murphy Brown, China Beach, L.A. Law, The Days and Nights of Molly Dodd* and *thirtysomething* came into being, signaling a move from programs simply marketed toward this post-war generation to shows explicitly about them.

The strategy of targeting specific audiences was an attempt to counteract the networks' loss of viewers to the burgeoning cable industry. All three networks lost 5 percent of their prime-time audience share in the 1989 season, for example, at which time their overall share of viewers had dropped to 62 percent of the viewing public (Auletta 1991:20). So, in part as an attempt to staunch the flow of viewers to cable, as well as to market their television "product" selectively to a specific niche rather than cast a wide net, programs like *thirtysomething* were given the go-ahead as a lure to the baby-boomers (Carter 1991: D1).[5]

Ultimately, although the network marketing strategy was intent on creating programs for certain niches of the market, they could not guarantee that the programs would be watched. For, with competition from cable and home video continuing to whittle away at network audiences, network television knew it would be increasingly difficult to get their audiences to stay with them for an entire evening. One strategy the networks began to pursue was to capture younger viewers who were not the privileged Yuppies of the *thirtysomething* genre. Such programs as *Roseanne* on ABC, as well as a grittier, working-class version of *thirtysomething* produced by Zwick and Herskovitz called *Dream Street* (jokingly referred to in the industry as *dirtysomething*), represented just such an attempt to attract a larger group of baby boomers (Gerard 1988:28).

In general, however, the networks have been playing a losing game, despite their different marketing strategies, as audiences shift and age and move around to different media (cable and video) to get their entertainment. In fact, some people have argued that marketing programs to younger viewers does not make sense any more because that historical age group is now part of the 35 to 54 age bracket (Carter 1991b:D1). In other words, the aging of the "boomers," who had been the primary market for ABC, means that these viewers have now been bumped into an older demographic grouping.

Despite the fact, then, that ABC had been pursuing a specific target marketing strategy for four years, by the summer of 1991 it had reversed its position and decided to cancel *thirtysomething*. Whereas the earlier strategy was on innovative shows addressed to specific demographic markets, the three networks, faced with shrinking advertising dollars and smaller budgets, reversed themselves and decided to produce much more conventional programs in the hopes of once again going for the mass market of earlier eras (Carter 1991a). Citing the fact that it was difficult to bear the burden of producing programs that were unprofitable, ABC canceled not only *thirtysomething* but two other shows that also appealed to the now aging boomers, *China Beach* and *Twin Peaks* (Carter 1991a). Because *thirtysomething*'s ratings fell that year from 12.3 to 10.6, and its audience now consisted primarily of younger women, its narrow demographics made it increasingly unattractive to a network seeking to boost ratings and increase viewers (Carter 1991a).

Instead of unconventional dramas, ABC added a number of new comedies.[6] *Thirtysomething* itself was replaced, not by a comedy, but by a show called *Home Front*, a drama about Americans in the years just following World War II. Though also a drama, the program was much more conventional in its storyline, about a historical period that gave birth, ironically enough, to the demographic group depicted on *thirtysomething*.

Television, Feminism, and the Cultural Backlash Against Women

While *thirtysomething*'s stories emerged from the artistic vision of its creators, Herskovitz and Zwick, the show may also be seen as arising within a televisual landscape that had closed off many of the more explicitly feminist concerns aired during the active phases of the women's movement in the 1970s. These concerns included questioning traditional roles for men and women, fighting for equal rights and relief for working mothers, and encouraging women to strike out on their own and develop themselves. As television scholar Ella Taylor has pointed out, many of the prime time shows of the 1970s, from *The Mary Tyler Moore Show* to *One Day at a Time* to *Maude* and even *All in the Family*, addressed themselves to women's new lives as a result of the women's movement, and as such arguably constituted a kind of "prime-time feminism" (Taylor 1989). This "feminism" was not without contradictions, of course. For example, the feminist impetus behind having Mary Tyler Moore shown as a single woman "making it on her own" was offset by her relationship with her male boss, played paternalistically by Ed Asner. But considering the prior silence of television on such issues, their representation did achieve a certain breakthrough.

In the 1980s, this prime-time feminism had been altered in the wake of a general re-questioning of many of the goals of the women's movement. Taylor notes that in such shows as *Cagney and Lacey*, *The Cosby*

Show, and *thirtysomething* women's roles were being seriously re-evaluated, with attention now being paid to the unintended costs of the women's movement. Looking specifically at *thirtysomething,* Taylor observes how the married female character Hope goes through tortured deliberations about whether to return to work after having her child, while the single characters are made out to be miserably unhappy because they do not have a husband or children. Taylor ultimately questions the feminist potential of programs such as *thirtysomething,* seeing in them only a kind of backlash against the women's movement (Taylor 1989:159).

In entering into contemporary discussions about gender and family through their portrayal of "real life," the creators of *thirtysomething* indirectly took up a position in the debate. This position, most scholars have agreed, is conservative in that it portrays more traditional roles for men and women as the most viable ones, even though most men and women cannot in fact reproduce these roles as they had in earlier eras (Loeb 1990; Taylor 1989; Hanke 1990; Torres 1989). Yet this may not be the whole story. While the text of *thirtysomething* can reasonably be described as part of a cultural backlash toward women, female viewers may not see themselves as part of this backlash. In fact, many of the viewers saw themselves as feminists, or at least as holding views long associated with feminism. Thus there is a gap between the critical interpretations of the show put forth by scholars and the experience of many women who were faithful viewers of the show.

This tension between viewpoints, between the ideas of critical media scholars and those of the female viewing audience, prompted me to explore this terrain in more detail. What did *thirtysomething* mean to its viewing audience? What themes about gender emerged and did they relate to conflicts in viewers' lives? How did women think and talk about fictional characters on a television show? And why did these characters feel so real to women?

Writing about female audiences and their use of popular romance novels, Janice Radway has pointed out that, in order to understand why romance novels sell so well, it is first important to know what a romance *is* for women who buy and read them (Radway 1984).[7] Following this lead, I interviewed female viewers of *thirtysomething* to try to understand what place the program had in their lives, why they watched it, and what meanings about gender, if any, they generated through the experience of viewing, thinking, and talking about it. During the 1990-1991 television season, I conducted interviews with twenty female viewers in the New York metropolitan area and handed out written questionnaires to another thirty women for a total of fifty respondents. I deliberately chose female viewers who belonged to the demographic group that the programmers of *thirtysomething* most wanted to reach: primarily white, middle-class Americans between the ages of twenty-five and forty-five. I wanted to see how it was true that a certain cultural text was able to "speak" to its intended audience in such a way as to elicit strong identifications on the part of the viewer.

The interviewed women lived in Brooklyn, Manhattan, and Staten Island, New York, and Princeton, New Jersey, and ranged in age from approximately twenty to forty-five. Slightly more than half were in their thirties. The majority of the women had attended some amount of college, and over a third were currently in school. Approximately half were married, and half were single, either never married or divorced. In addition, at least a third of the women had children and over three-quarters were planning to have them.

Female Viewers and Social Class

A number of scholars have tried to come to terms with the complex nature of assigning a class status to an individual. Some have utilized Marxist approaches, which locate class primarily in relation to the means of production, and look at the job the individual occupies in a capitalist society (Bottomore 1983; Parkin 1979). Feminist scholars, too, have entered the debate. Writers such as Mary Ryan (1979) and Ann Oakley (1974) argue that women's specific work under capitalism casts doubt on the notion that women simply belong to their husbands' class. These writers instead view women in a capitalist society as potentially having more in common with one another than with the class of their husbands. Other feminists, including Kate Millett (1971), argue that women perhaps themselves make up a separate class altogether in our society, and challenge the very notion of class based on economic, status, or prestige as ignoring the fundamental division in society between men and women.

Given the as yet unresolved debate about how to determine an individual's class background, the most reasonable strategy for my study seemed to lie in combining a number of traditional sociological variables for a comprehensive portrait of an individual woman's class affiliation. Thus I began my investigation by looking at the occupations of the women (and their husbands if they were married) as well as those of their parents. I also included the women's income level, whether they were professionals or skilled or non-skilled workers, how much disposable income they had, how much property they owned, their educational status and aspirations, where they lived and how much money, if any, they had saved.

The responses yielded some interesting differences in terms of individuals' sense of whether they had the same life options as the female characters on *thirtysomething*. Lower-middle-class women felt that they did not have the same opportunities to make the kinds of decisions that the female characters often did. In addition, lower-middle-class women tended not to identify so much with the female characters as with the *situations* these characters found themselves in. Often, they were annoyed with the female characters themselves, seeing them as a bunch of whining "yuppies." At the same time, however, they found that the situations these yuppies were in were similar to situations they were facing in their own lives: the division of labor at home, trying to meet men, spending enough time with their children, and so on. For this reason, while lower-middle-class women tended to judge the female characters more harshly than did their upper-middle-class counterparts, they nevertheless "bonded" to these characters in terms of the situations that were depicted. More provocatively, they often used these characters to define their own class limits and horizons, by saying what they would do if they had the same privileges as the upper- middle-class female characters. In this way, class may be understood as a lived category for the lower- and upper-middle-class women; in a sense they constituted and re-affirmed themselves as class subjects in part through their interaction with the program.

Upper-middle-class women too used *thirtysomething* as a springboard for articulating not only their gender conflicts but also their lives as upper-middle-class women. That is, they tended to use the program to affirm some of the life choices they had made as women who were privileged and had the option, say, to leave their job if it conflicted with the demands of home. In addition, they tended to identify with and draw on the language (or "whining") that the female characters used to describe their conflicts, and were much less put off by the class privileges that this verbalizing seemed to imply to the lower-middle-class women. Upper-middle-class women felt entitled, in other words, to complain about their lives, even when those lives seemed privileged to someone looking at them from the outside. In addition, they also felt comfortable with the therapeutic aspects of verbalizing discontent, while the lower-middle-class women tended to resent women who seemingly had it all but nevertheless felt the need to complain.

How the Interviews Were Conducted

Given the limited number, geographic location, and age of the women I spoke with, I am not seeking to make claims about all female viewers of *thirtysomething.* Rather, my aim is to understand how one demographically "desirable" group generates meaning. If my subjects' responses yield more general insights into the way middle-class white women who watch popular tv narratives use them, it is because I sought more in-depth interviews rather than a broader and more representative sample. Following the research of other feminist scholars, including Lillian Rubin (1976), Carol Stack (1974), and Andrea Press (1991), I adopted the method of snowball sampling, whereby I first located one woman who was a regular viewer and then asked her for names of other women she knew who also watched the show regularly (See Rubin 1976). In some cases, I established contact with clusters of friends through this approach. This approach had important consequences for the research, for the women often would refer to one another as they tried to describe other people's reactions to the show. In such cases, they frequently offered their opinions about how their friends "matched up" with the characters on the program. I would then go to meet the woman who was described as being "just like Melissa," perhaps to find that she described her friend as being "a clone of Hope!" This method enabled me to chart the ways not just individual women but informal networks of friends made deliberate and not-so-deliberate use of the show.

In all, I interviewed six clusters of friends. I recruited the starting persons for the snowball clusters from a community college in Staten Island and from a white working-class and middle-class New York City neighborhood in Brooklyn called Park Slope, which was part of the gentrification process in the 1980s and was therefore known as a somewhat "yuppified" area. In addition, I conducted interviews with a cluster of lower-middle- and middle-class secretaries at a law firm in the Wall Street area of Manhattan and upper-middle-class lawyers, with another cluster of middle-class women from a non-profit educational institution in New York City, and with a cluster of upper-middle-class women from a well-to-do suburban community in Princeton, New Jersey. The final cluster was composed of single middle-class women, again from Park Slope. Each interview lasted about two hours and was followed up by one more interview, where additional questions were posed to fill in the gaps. About one third of the interviews were held in groups where the participants knew one another; the remainder were held individually.

The interviews took place in a variety of locations—at home, at work, in coffee shops, on stoops in neighborhoods of Brooklyn, in backyards in the suburbs. Almost invariably the women had a surprising amount to say about the show and were able to recall the details of scenes and even dialogue not just from the most recent episode but from those that had aired weeks and sometimes months earlier. Most commonly, I would not watch the show with the women, but would try to meet with them on the day after the show had aired.[8]

Some of the most enjoyable interviews took place away from the women's homes or offices; we might meet for lunch and sit outside, or take a walk, or go for a cup of coffee. The spring and summer months, when most of the interviews were conducted, were conducive to interviewing in outside spaces, such as the sidewalks along Broadway, the Brooklyn and Manhattan promenades, the peaceful backyards of Princeton, and the stoops of Park Slope. Mostly, the women seemed to enjoy the process of self-reflection, the opportunity to "vent" about the problems in their lives, as well as to "dish" with another viewer about the goings on of the program. I did not hesitate to enter into sympathetic reflections with interviewees, and often shared aspects of my own life with them, but I avoided making specific comments on the show or its characters. The conversations were gratifying for me as well as to the interviewees. Even when our experiences and perspectives diverged significantly, we often found common ground with one another, suspending for a moment the pressures of work and family challenges.

Identification: Fusing Fantasy and Reality

I will claim that the female viewers of *thirtysomething* did in fact identify with the conflicts, desires, dreams, and frustrations of the female characters. But what does it mean to "identify" with a tv character? The sense in which I am using the term "identification" derives from other studies of female viewership. Ien Ang, for example, uses the term 'identification' to describe how female viewers tended to adopt symbolically the various "subject" positions of the female characters on the television program *Dallas*. According to Ang, *Dallas* was successful because it was able to create female characters onto whom female viewers could project simultaneously, in positive and negative ways, their own lives (Ang 1990:83). These projections were "experienced as moments of peace, of truth, of redemption, a moment in which the complexity of the task of being a woman is fully realised and accepted" (Ang 1990:86–87).

Ang's work is perhaps most important because she raises the issue of why women derive pleasure from identifying with characters who are often pathetic, evil, or simply unlucky, as when she describes the "tragic structure of feeling" that allows women to identify with the crises of other female characters which in turn acts as a catharsis or release of their own feelings (Ang 1985:21).[9] Other writers in the cultural studies tradition, such as Cora Kaplan in her work on *The Thorn Birds,* have also identified pleasure as a key component in women's use of popular culture, and have explicitly raised the issue of how fantasy is a central element, in addition to one's class and gender position, in determining meanings (C. Kaplan 1986).

Complex forms of identification can also be found in African-American female responses to the film *The Color Purple.* Jacqueline Bobo explored the problem of how African-American women, despite the stereotypical and negative portrayals in the film, could nevertheless "negotiate" or come away with positive identifications with the female characters in the film. Part of the reason viewers identified with the characters was that they perceived it as part of a larger cultural renaissance among black women writers. In this sense, Stephen Spielberg, the director of the film *The Color Purple,* benefited from the fact that Alice Walker, the writer of the book *The Color Purple,* was seen within a larger cultural milieu that the viewers were excited about. These viewers felt that this cultural renaissance was a means by which their own stories as African-American women would finally be told (Bobo 1988:101).

A final example of the complex ways in which female viewers identify with characters from popular culture can be seen in Andrea Press's study *Women Watching Television* (Press 1991). Press found that middle-class women, for example, while more self-conscious about the constructed nature of the medium than working-class women, nevertheless identified with many television characters. She found that these middle-class viewers related to television characters in what she terms "gender specific" ways, focusing on the "interpersonal" themes in the program and forming identifications with characters on the basis of their sense that they shared a common "women's culture" (Press 1991:66–67).[10] More generally, identification can be understood as a reciprocal process: viewers enter imaginatively into the world of a fictional character or characters; and characters become emotional reference points in the real lives of viewers. Identification, then, has an emotional as well as a cognitive basis.

The fact that women found *thirtysomething* realistic, furthermore, even while they recognized some parts as fantastic, underscores a more general problem with the common dichotomy between realism and fantasy. Andrea Press found that middle-class female viewers of *Dynasty,* for example, while recognizing the overall unreality of a program about fabulously rich people, nevertheless identified with precisely these characters (Press 1991). Likewise, in their study of African-American and white viewers of *The Cosby Show,* Sut Jhally and Justin Lewis (1992) have remarked on the seemingly contradictory attitude that both these groups display toward the "reality" of the show. While the majority of their respondents were aware that most African Americans do not lead the privileged lives of the Cosbys, they continually mixed fiction and reality in their glowing descriptions of the show as "realistic" (Jhally and Lewis 1992:20). Jhally and Lewis attribute this to the fact that television characters come into our homes on a regular basis, perhaps more regularly than the real people in our lives. This creates a sense of familiarity not only with the characters but with the entire "world" of the program:

> Television allows us to regularly invite a select group of people into our homes. Though most of these people are fictional characters, their regular visits create a sense of familiarity that is hard to resist.... Once we allow ourselves this degree of familiarity, it is possible to see how fantasy and reality fade quietly into one another, how our TV friends and acquaintances take their place within our "real" world and jostle for attention and support with our "real" friends and family. This blurring of the distinction between fantasy and everyday life was a constant feature of nearly all our respondents' comments. (Jhally and Lewis 1992:18–19)

Like the viewers of *The Cosby Show, Dynasty,* and *Dallas,* the women I interviewed allowed the characters into their lives, formed identifications with many of them, and used them to think about their own gender conflicts. In fact, it became clear that, far more than other shows they watched regularly, *thirtysomething* held a distinct place in the lives of these viewers. Because the characters served as mouthpieces for various conflicts women have over men, families, jobs, and other friends, they seemed to most women to have more impact than people they knew, who did not verbalize their problems with such ease. Characters, in other words, have more influence than people's own friends, in terms of their capacity to provoke them to think and reflect about life choices. This accords with Jhally and Lewis's finding that the characters on *The Cosby Show* often felt like better friends to their viewers than their own friends.

More generally, the fictional characters of *thirtysomething* ended up serving as emotional soundboards, resonating women's crises back to them each week in a safe, contained environment that could then be shut off until the next program. In this way, *thirtysomething* helped to serve, as Sasha Torres (1989) and Robert Hanke (1990) have noted, as a kind of therapeutic device for women, and drew on many of the discourses of the therapeutic culture as a way to draw viewers into the drama of their "everyday" lives.

Mass Culture and Female Audience Reception: Woman as Gendered Subjects

The meanings women viewers made of *thirtysomething*, then, were not strictly up to them. Their interpretations were an active negotiation of the media text, their own lived experience and personal histories, and the historically determined discourses and ideologies—shared ways of making sense of things like tv shows and relationships—that were available in the dominant culture. Each of these elements that are fused in the act of reading, history, text, and lived experience must be examined for its influence on the meanings made. And the act of reading itself transforms each of these in turn. But on what terms should such an examination proceed?

In this book I draw on recent scholarship in feminist media criticism, psychoanalytic theory, sociology of culture, cultural studies, and postmodern theory. Each of these has important empirical and theoretical insights to contribute to our understanding of the ways people make individual and collective sense of cultural artifacts and their own lives. After briefly reviewing some of the dominant trends that characterize research on women and popular culture, I will then turn to recent developments in postmodern and cultural theory as it pertains to audience reception. As will be shown, my research on female viewers of *thirtysomething* draws on the important insights generated within these traditions about how individuals use popular culture to construct particular meanings about themselves.

Only recently have scholars begun to study how meanings about gender are embedded in popular media and interpreted by female viewers (E. Kaplan 1987). Such studies emerged in the late 1960s and 1970s in response to women's changing position in society and, with it, the new influx of women scholars into the academy.[11] The first research paradigm in this period used content analysis to catalogue the images of women that appeared in prominent films and tv programs. Some studies were in the tradition of mainstream social science, essentially counting the incidence of different kinds of programs (Tuchman 1978; Courtney and Whipple 1980; Butler and Paisley 1980). Similar studies in the field of feminist film and television criticism catalogued changing stereotypes of women in different historical periods (M. Haskell 1987; M. Rosen 1973).

One example of the "images of women" approach is Diana Meehan's *Ladies of the Evening: Women Characters of Prime-Time Television* (1983). Meehan examines the roles in which female characters appear, the number of violent acts committed against them, and the number of jokes made about them, as well as a host of other factors. She also charts changes in the kinds of female roles shown on night-time television from 1950 to 1980. Throughout this period, she finds that female characters with pursuits outside the home are portrayed in service roles of one kind or another and that the women shown as wage-earners are single rather than married women. Popular television narratives, she concludes, thereby reinforced the real bifurcation of women into married housewives and single workers.

While these quantitative studies of "images of women" are helpful in telling us about television's changing portrayals of women, they are limited because they do not begin to explore the complex ways in which audiences interpret and respond to these images. Furthermore, given the multi-valent meanings of even the most straightforward representation, it is doubtful that a simple classificatory rubric is adequate even as content analysis. If one finds, for example, that there are fifty-four themes devoted to women's equality on network television in a given year, this finding only gives us the general impression of the programming and tells us nothing about how the issue of gender equality is portrayed, what the tensions are, who is speaking about this equality, what the context of the portrayal is, what sense the audience makes of this theme, how contradictory the message may be in relation to other plot developments and characters, and so on. There are a whole host of important questions that cannot be answered simply by counting the number of themes devoted to women's equality on network television.

Other feminist work in gender and mass culture has responded to the limitations of the "images of women" approach by developing a more sophisticated reading of mass cultural narratives themselves. One of the most important developments in feminist film criticism was its adoption of psychoanalytic theory for both a reading of mass cultural narratives and an analysis of the relationship between a film or television "text" and its spectator (see Flitterman-Lewis 1987:172–211). Psychoanalytic theory offered a rich account of the social construction of sexual (gender) differences and as such promised to be a fruitful set of tools for many feminist scholars who were trying to think about how "gendered" viewers were positioned for understanding mass cultural artifacts. For example, through such writers as Freud and later Jacques Lacan, Julia Kristeva, and Nancy Chodorow, identification with familial figures and symbolically meaningful persons are seen as integral to the individual's ability to form a social identity (Kristeva 1976; Chodorow 1978). Later film theorists such as Christian Metz (1982), Kaja Silverman (1983),

Teresa de Lauretis (1984), and Mary Ann Doane (1987), among others, took this paradigm of identification and tried to apply it to the process of film spectatorship, exploring how individuals form powerful identifications with film and television characters, much as children form their social identities through symbolic identification with parental and caregiving figures; moreover, film and television could be said to *position* the spectator, as if in a dream, to 'read' the film a certain way.

One highly influential essay that discussed the specific issue of film spectatorship and sexual difference was Laura Mulvey's "Visual Pleasure and Narrative Cinema" (1975). Mulvey draws on the Freudian concepts of fetishism and voyeurism to describe the ways in which Hollywood films, in their formal construction, are geared toward the unconscious desires of the male spectator. The conclusion of this essay, which shaped a decade of feminist media scholarship, was that classical Hollywood cinema denies women's subjectivity through its exclusive emphasis on the "male" gaze. By this Mulvey means that films are essentially structured to satisfy the psychic needs of male viewers, who can watch a film in the dark from a distance, with a male point of view and a male narrative. Although there were and still are a genre of "women's films," which instead emphasize a female viewpoint and draw the (female) viewer in through melodramatic narratives that connect the viewer to the drama, for the most part Hollywood films focused on male themes with a male point of view.

Part of the problem with this framework, which later theorists including Mulvey pointed out, was that, in relying on classical Freudian theory, it focused too exclusively on the male psyche and left little room for theorizing female spectatorship. In part in response to these initial formulations, more recent feminist psychoanalytic cultural theory has begun to theorize about the unconscious processes of female spectators. For example, Tania Modleski (1981) has utilized the theories of Nancy Chodorow (1978) and Luce Irigaray (1980) to explore how the soap opera relies on a sense of "nearness" to its female spectator, which in turn allows women to re-experience the intimacy they supposedly shared with their mothers in early childhood. Charlotte Brunsdon (1983) adds sociological analysis to a psychoanalytic approach by relating the structure of the British soap opera *Crossroads* to the socialized needs of a female audience. In particular, she argues that the "ideal" spectator films construct is a socialized spectator, and she develops a persuasive account of the ways mass cultural products respond to women's socialized needs for intimacy and closeness.

The work of Jackie Byars (1988) and Patricia Mellencamp (1986) is also illuminating because they use psychoanalytic theory to look at historically specific texts, and they try to understand how the psychological needs of the spectator are rooted in a psyche that is itself embedded in a specific social and historical milieu. Mellencamp employs Freud's theory of jokes to understand how 1950s situation comedies such as *I Love Lucy* and *The George Burns and Gracie Allen Show* could appeal to both male and female spectators while at the same time admonishing dissatisfied females to remain at home. Byars also has done important work with psychoanalytic theory, in this case employing Nancy Chodorow's (1978) theories on female bonding to analyze how the plots of certain female-oriented melodramas from the 1950s may have responded to women's desires for intense female friendships.

A weakness of psychoanalytic theory is that in positing unconscious processes as primary, it tends to be ahistorical. Media theorists have responded by taking into account the sociological and historical aspects of female spectatorship as well as psychoanalytic accounts of gendered spectators. Attempting to rectify these gaps in contextualization, many recent scholars in film and television theory have begun to explore how a text, as well as a spectator, are embedded within a specific social and historical milieu. Linda Williams (1988), for example, examines the historical situation of female viewers of the 1940s, and argues that their experiences during World War II may have affected their reading of such movies as the 1945 "women's film" *Mildred Pierce.* Jeanne Allen (1988), in her analysis of *Rear Window,* suggests that female audiences may have responded differently to Hollywood cinema before and after the women's liberation era.

Both Allen's work and Williams's are useful because they emphasize the historically specific nature of meaning construction in mass culture. Rather than posit a fixed, ahistorical female "subject," these writers emphasize how the relationship between audience and text must be situated in order to be understood. Furthermore, by demonstrating how differently situated readers bring away different readings from a text, they implicitly challenge the notion that the text affects the spectator in a one-way relationship, and instead point to the ways in which the texts, viewers, and history are mutually determining.

Television, Postmodernity, and the "Death of the Subject"

Theories of postmodernity offer another useful set of resources for thinking about issues of audience reception and meaning. Postmodern theory questions the notion of personal subjectivity as something fixed and stable or even changeable and constructed. For example, writers on postmodernity such as Baudrillard (1983), Kroker and Cook (1986), and Deleuze and Guattari (1977) have, in various ways, critiqued the modern idea that an individual subject could be autonomous and self-creating. For these writers, personal identity is a kind of fiction or creation of language and society, one that "moderns" use to comfort themselves into thinking that the world is stable and orderly with an autonomous individual at the center of it. In contrast, postmodern theory introduces the notion of identity as "imploded" and unstable in a postmodern world which is itself undergoing a permanent state of change and transformation. Television, as writers like Baudrillard would have it, is a "simulacrum" or virtual reality whose narratives participate in the fiction that there are stable identities that can be represented in a realist format, while its *form* reflects the fragmentation and dislocation of social life. So, for postmodernist theorists, identity is a fiction and the social is dead. This implies that subjectivity and agency are refused by individual television viewers to somehow freely create their own subjectivity.

For other media scholars who use some of the theories of postmodernity, on the other hand, there is an understanding of personal identity as something that is real and constituted by subjects but nevertheless unstable. The major distinction between these theorists and the earlier postmodern theorists is the way in which the human subject as *agent* is theorized. Countering these ideas about television as pure images that are beamed out to televisual subjects who are themselves laboring under the illusion of having a fixed identity, recent writers have instead focused on the way television participates in the construction of our social identities (Kellner 1992:148). Douglas Kellner, for example, has suggested that television may be assuming some of the roles that myth and ritual played in pre-modern societies, by helping to integrate individuals into the social order as well as by offering models about appropriate behaviors, ideas, and values. Following Roland Barthes and Claude Lévi-Strauss, Kellner also describes the ways television helps to provide useful fictions or "mythologies" to help individuals resolve contemporary anxieties over their continually shifting identities. Although television helps to create our social selves, then, by providing us with various gender and role models, because there is such a tremendous variety of images to respond to in a postmodern culture, individuals may have to accept the instability of their identities in a way our pre-modern and modern ancestors were spared. As Kellner concludes:

> Rather than identity disappearing in a postmodern society, it is

> merely subject to new determinations and new forces while offering as well new possibilities, styles, models, and forms. Yet the overwhelming variety of subject positions, of possibilities for identity, in an affluent image culture no doubt create highly unstable identities while constantly providing new openings to restructure one's identity. (Kellner 1992:174)

Michel Foucault, while not writing specifically about popular culture, also reflects at length on the ways in which culture participates in the construction of our social identities. In such works as *Discipline and Punish* (1979), *Madness and Civilization* (1973), and Volume I of *The History of Sexuality* (1980), Foucault examines the way modern subjectivity has been constructed by institutional practices such as prisons, asylums, psychiatry, and schooling, which elaborate forms of knowledge that are simultaneously forms of self-knowledge. While Foucault has also written as though the self in modernity is a fiction, his writings suggest that culture forces a fixed identity onto what is a relatively fluid subjectivity. This imposition, characteristic of popular cultural artifacts as well, structure the individual's self-understanding. The recent self-help literature, with discourses of individuals as "victims," "survivors," "adult children of alcoholics," and so on might be one example of how forms of cultural knowledge become internalized and experienced as a core of one's identity. In these ways, both Foucault and Kellner point to how culture imposes identities in postmodern society.

Television and the Question of "Reality"

Another challenge raised by postmodernist reflections on culture concerns television's status as a realistic medium. One of the primary claims of Edward Zwick and Marshall Herskovitz, the creators of *thirtysomething*, is that their program mirrors the real-life experiences of their audience. Such claims presuppose, first, that there is something that can be called "real life" to begin with, instead of a series of fictions and, second, that television can offer a relatively unmediated picture of social reality to its viewers. On the contrary, television cannot be construed as offering such a picture because of the very constructed nature of the medium. John Fiske refers to this as the "transparency fallacy," as if television were somehow able simply to represent, without human agency, what is happening in society (cited in Seiter et al. 1989:21). Ella Taylor (1989) has also criticized the belief that television can act as a direct reflection, or "mirror," of society.

Postmodern theory in general would question the capacity of television, or any medium, to present a direct picture of social reality. This view is not unique to postmodern theory. What is unique is the belief that there is no "social reality." The boundaries of this, and the boundaries of "television," are elusive for postmodernists. Television, in this view, does not offer something called "social reality," but rather a crazy-quilt clash of representations, with no possibility of making sense. In much postmodern theory, then, the whole mode of representational realism that defines a great deal of what is seen on contemporary television is perceived as a fiction. These fictions are produced through narratives and stories that, as Kellner points out, are familiar and recognizable to the viewing population, who then perceive them to be accurate representations of social reality.

Much of the recent writing that borrows on postmodernist ideas questions the notion that television texts are somehow organically distinct from their viewers. In postmodern theory popular culture is understood as a "site" where viewers derive multiple meanings about their social selves by internalizing the discourses in the larger culture. Some writers, in their adoption of postmodernist ideas about televisual meanings, go so far as to challenge the very distinction between television and audiences altogether, instead positing a social world that is "intertextual," that is, where individuals create their social selves through processes such as viewing television, which itself contains no one determinate meaning. Writers such as John Fiske propose that the categories "the text" and "the audience" themselves be abolished, or rather collapsed. As he explains, the television audience is not itself a social group who can be easily identified, precisely because there can be no "meaningful categories beyond its boundaries—what on earth is not the television audience?" (in Seiter et al. 1989:56). The television text, in the same way, is such an expansive category that it is almost impossible to define. There is no way one could identify, for example, one simple message that will be received in the same way by disparate audiences. I believe these critiques of television and audiences are valid, and help us to understand that meanings that are derived from television must always be perceived as contingent and open-ended.

Ultimately, it is important to retain the concept of discrete texts and audiences, however, because there are groups of people who can be identified who watch certain programs that can also be identified. That being said, I do believe that the postmodernist challenge to the unified subjectivity of modernity has important implications for thinking about television viewing. The understanding of individual subjectivity as being formed through the subjects in cultural practices does not, however, have to be understood deterministically in the sense that individuals are seen as wholly determined by the texts of culture. Rather, it should simply point out how we, as subjects, can become subject to the dominant meanings in the larger culture. The viewer has the freedom to "activate" one set of meanings over another. These activations, however, are determined to some extent by the social locations of the particular viewers, that is, how they have already been constituted as viewing subjects through their social position in late capitalism. All in all, postmodernist theory offers a vision of a social world of radically shifting subjectivities that interact with popular culture to acquire new social identities that will in turn help them adapt to the larger sea changes transpiring in society.

Finally, postmodern theory has much to say not only about the genre of realism but about television's claim to represent faithfully the social reality of its viewers. In the Baudrillardian universe, not only television but all social reality exists as a kind of simulacrum; there is no "out there." The realism of television is merely a chimera mimicking the non-reality of the social world, which is ever changing and mutating in our rapidly shifting historical juncture.

I do not adopt the postmodern, Baudrillardian view of television as part of a simulacrum in postmodern society, flashing mimetic images in a sea of white noise. Postmodern critiques of television's realism are useful, though, for they challenge us to think critically about any television show that claims to portray the "real life" of its viewers, a group who may have had radically disparate experiences from one another. Perhaps the best way to understand the realism of television shows like *thirtysomething* is to say that it presents a conflictual view of social reality, which viewers then watch to help them make sense, somehow, of their own world. It is that "somehow" that I will interrogate in this study of female viewers of *thirtysomething*.

Cultural Studies Approaches

In addition to these theories of media reception, another important theoretical approach that explores the question of meaning in popular culture is what has come to be known as the cultural studies approach, a Marxist-inspired cultural analysis introduced by Stuart Hall, Tony Bennett, David Morley, and others at the Birmingham Centre for Cultural Studies in England (Morley 1989; Gurevitch et al. 1982). Drawing on the work of American anthropologist Dell Hymes (1972) and French sociologist Pierre Bourdieu (1984), among others, these scholars try to understand how audiences interpret a cultural product according to their place in the social order.

Mary Ann Moffitt has drawn a useful distinction between two operative models of British cultural studies. The first theory of communication they offer is an "encoding-decoding" model, which emphasizes the viewers' class position, gender, and lived experience as integral to their decoding of a particular media product (Moffitt 1993). An example is David Morley's study of family viewing habits of the British television program *Nationwide.* Morley examines the social position of men and women in families as integral to their construction of meaning about television programs (Morley 1986). He finds that men and women may have different strategies of viewing, with men dominating the choice of program through monopolizing the technology itself, while women move in and out of viewing as they also try to accomplish chores around the house. Thus for women television viewing, because it occurs at home, where they are also responsible for household labor, is continually subject to interruption. A further elaboration of the "encoding-decoding" model can be found in the work of Angela McRobbie, who looks at how British female teenagers use such cultural artifacts as magazines and dance to define themselves (McRobbie 1980, 1982a, 1982b, 1984). For example, female teenagers draw on dance as a means of articulating their burgeoning sexuality and helping to construct a particular version of femininity that will be used to attract men. McRobbie's work is important because it raises the problem of how gender is as important a factor in how individuals construct meanings as their class position.

The second model employed by the British cultural theorists is the articulation model (Hall 1986). This model moves beyond the idea that the viewer's class or gender position alone determines the meanings that are made of the text. The articulation model instead posits that meaning is determined by the intersection ("articulation") of various ideologies within the viewer's social experiences, including both individual and social factors. As Moffitt points out, "Hall's articulation model views meaning as an historical moment in which cultural forces, textual features, and social pressures on the individual receiver all intersect and articulate meaning to the receiver" (Moffitt 1993:234).This interpretation moves us beyond the increasingly sterile debate over the power of the text versus the power of the audience in the creation of meaning. For in the articulation model meaning is the result of myriad intersecting factors, many of which are contradictory, including, as Moffitt writes, "the fantasy of the text; the ideologically and culturally charged social, gender and labor positions of the receiver; and currently felt, so-called 'real' lived experience of the receiver" (Moffitt 1993:235).

Recent work on television that borrows from cultural studies has explored the complex social act involved in television viewing, and focused on audience reactions as well as the "texts" or television programs themselves. This dual emphasis on "texts" and "audiences" is vital because television's meanings are never completely open to a reader's interpretation; nor are they completely closed off, or determined by the text itself (Morley 1989). In addition to the text and audience, cultural studies approaches scrutinize the economic and institutional circumstances that give rise to the text. Todd Gitlin (1987), for example, has pointed out in his work on prime-time television that it is necessary to look in detail at how television shows are produced as well as how they are consumed.

In order to explore how women respond to and use popular culture to help make sense of their lives, feminist scholars in the cultural studies tradition have adopted the use of in-depth interviews as a means of understanding the group they are studying (Press 1989; Bobo 1988). This work, which might be termed "feminist ethnography," seeks to understand how women use the products of mass culture in the construction of what might be termed "woman's culture."

Janice Radway's work on female audiences is a good illustration of this kind of approach (Radway 1987). In studying women's use of romance novels in the United States, Radway has demonstrated how women use popular culture to constitute a specifically female subjectivity. These subjectivities are formed both in resistance to the meanings inherent in the texts of popular culture and arguably in reinforcement of them. For Radway, activities such as romance reading connect with women's need to express their sexuality and open up fantasies of alternative forms of desire and intimacy. The larger point is that, unlike traditional psychoanalytic or Marxist theorists, these feminist ethnographers emphasize the dialectical nature of female subjectivity as a product both of the larger cultural representations of femininity and of resistances to those representations. In this view, women use popular culture to try and make sense of their situation and to constitute a female subjectivity.

Framework of This Study

My approach in this book is guided by parts of all these theories, and in particular the cultural studies approach, with its threefold emphasis on text, audience, and history. In this way, I have tried to bridge an increasingly widening gap in media studies between those who would seek to analyze either the texts or the audiences to the exclusion of one another. Focusing on one program, rather than an entire genre or population, allowed such an integrated approach to work.

My guiding assumption during these interviews was that it is impossible to determine whether a television show is "really" realistic, primarily because there is no social reality "out there" that is not somehow mediated by our perceptions of it. Because of my skepticism about the project of measuring *thirtysomething* against an unmediated social reality outside television, I was more concerned with the ways in which *thirtysomething* related to its female viewers' sense of reality. What was it about the show, if anything, that felt "true to life" to these women? My discussion has three parts therefore: the social, historical, and economic milieu in which *thirtysomething* came into being; an analysis of how *thirtysomething* presented gender issues; and finally, discussions of tv meanings female viewers made about their own gender identities.

As stated earlier, *thirtysomething* arose within a very specific business context of network television. During this period all three networks were undergoing tremendous shifts and strains as a result of changing demographic and audience shares. *Thirtysomething* represented one particular marketing strategy to capture the newly segmented market group of baby boomers, and its life and death as a prime-time network program was dependent on the sea changes transpiring in the media business during the late 1980s.

As an historical artifact, *thirtysomething* emerged at a time when a number of discussions were taking place that questioned the original goals of the women's movement and chastised feminists for ignoring women's desires to hold on to some of their earlier social roles as wives and mothers. *Thirtysomething* drew on these discussions in representing women's role conflicts on the show, and implicitly challenged assumptions about what was politically "correct" and "incorrect" as to what roles women should play out in their family lives. To illuminate this process, this study undertakes a critical analysis of the female characters of *thirtysomething*, to see how the program illustrated the conflicts women have in playing out one role over another. As will be shown, the women in the show are divided into camps by virtue of roles they play out, serving as symbolic embodiments of the choices supposedly available to women today.

Chapter 3 offers a critical reading of several episodes of *thirtysomething*. This analysis tracks themes that relate directly to the representation of women's gender conflicts, including threats to the domestic sphere, reconciliation with motherhood, and conflicts over work and family. As we will see, the plotlines of the weekly stories, while demonstrating the conflicts in painful detail, often resolve the characters' difficulties in such a way as to affirm the primacy of traditional gender roles. I will argue that these stories end up serving as a kind of morality tale to caution women against deviating too strongly from traditional roles, even though most of the viewers were in fact already deviating in important ways.

The third part of the study includes interviews with female viewers of *thirtysomething* as a means of exploring tensions between the resolutions of the narratives and their own lives. I was particularly interested in finding out viewers' reactions to the purported realism of the program, as well as their responses to the portrayal of gender role conflicts.

Tania Modleski, reacting to the new emphasis on empirical audience studies inaugurated by the British cultural studies tradition, has argued that there is a continuing need to "adopt a more critical view of mass cultural productions and mass cultural artifacts, one in particular that would concentrate on texts without, however, disregarding contexts," in order to retain a critical stance toward the texts, which is often not available through a primary emphasis on audiences' interpretation (Modleski 1986:xiii). This study of *thirtysomething* represents an attempt to address Modleski's concern with an overemphasis on audience reactions by precisely exploring the texts and contexts of a widely viewed network program.

It is my hope that this study will be instructive not only to feminist theorists, who are trying to address contemporary women's concerns and anxieties over their changing gender roles, but to other practitioners in the field of media studies, who are trying to come to terms with the complex problematic of how meanings are constructed in mass culture.

Notes

1. Included in the liberal vision is the idea that more than one type of family exists, with extended generations, same-sex partners, single parents, and divorced partners all viewed as all having the potential to be loving caregivers. It also recognizes that both men and women have to work in today's economy, for financial and personal reasons, and that gender roles should be open enough to reflect these economic realities.

2. Marshall Herskovitz and Edward Zwick, the co-creators of *thirtysomething*, make reference to their desire to create a program about the "real life" of the thirtysomething generation. For a good discussion of this goal, which characterizes a number of programs in this genre, see their Introduction in *Thirtysomething Stories* (Zwick and Herskovitz 1991:3–9).

3. Eleanor Blau, for example, reporting for the *New York Times*, found that the viewers identified with the characters and that the characters' lives seemed to mirror the lives of many in the baby boom generation. She also found that the core viewers were women between 18 and 34 years old, followed closely by men of the same age and women 35 to 49 (Blau 1990:C14).

4. For an interesting discussion of the marketing aspects of shows such as *thirtysomething*, see Gerard 1988:28.

5. Perhaps because of this marketing strategy on the part of ABC, it had not led the household ratings race for more than ten years, as Bill Carter goes on to point out. However, it had been the leader in attracting young adult viewers, which meant that while it lost the so-called "ratings game" it actually *won* in terms of the overall category of profits generated from advertisers, who wanted to go after this group. ABC earned about $220 million in 1991 with this demographic strategy, while NBC brought in only about $50 million (Carter 1991b:D1). As executives such as Brandon Tartikoff, formerly of NBC, have conceded, the biggest catch remains the approximately 75 million baby-boomer viewers. To develop shows that would appeal to this group, furthermore, he believed was in some sense an easier task, because the majority of the staff working in television at that time was precisely in this age group (Gerard 1988:28).

6. For example, listing the new shows, ABC offered such fare in place of shows like *thirtysomething* as *Home Improvements*, a comedy about a home repairs expert; *Grown-ups*, a comedy starring Marsha Mason; *Good and Evil*, a satire about twins with opposite natures; *Bird and Katt*, the previous year's *Gabriel's Fire* reworked as an action-comedy; *Step by Step*, a comedy about newlyweds, with Suzanne Somers and Patrick Duffy; *F.B.I: The Untold Stories*, a "reality" series with stories from the files; and *The Commish*, a drama about a tough police commissioner (Carter 1991a:48).

7. As she continues, "To know that, we must know what romance readers make of the words they find on the page; we must know, in short, how they construct the plot and interpret the characters' intentions" (Radway 1987:11).

8. Many of the interviews were interrupted, because the woman had to go back to work or make dinner or whatever. We would then resume at a later point, picking up where we left off, More than once this left me with the eerie sense that the research itself was mirroring the show, since this pattern of interrupted and resumed conversations was characteristic of the show's portrayal of the harried domestic and work lives of thirtysomethings. When I interviewed people at work, there were even

more restrictions in terms of time, so I sometimes had to cut short interesting discussions in order to allow enough time to cover all my interview questions.

9. Citing Pierre Bourdieu's notion of "the aristocracy of culture" (Bourdieu 1980), Ang notes that most forms of popular pleasure involve some kind of emotional or sensual involvement with the object; that is, people try to identify with the object in some way. This process of recognition in turn is what constitutes the pleasure for most viewers (Ang 1990:83).

10. In thinking through the results of how middle-class women *respond* to the interpersonal and gender-specific issues raised by the female characters on television, Press goes on to report that middle-class women are apparently conflicted between two "ideals" for women, one reflecting a culturally "feminist" emphasis on independence, autonomy, and the pursuit of a career and the other valorizing the more traditional female goals of finding fulfillment through a husband and family (Press 1991:81). These conflicted responses account for why middle-class women, unlike their working-class counterparts, were able to identify with such disparate female images as the "assertive housewife, the independent feminist, and the sexy glamour-girl" (Press 1991:83). By contrast, working-class female viewers tended to have more negative reactions to the "feminist" ideal of certain television characters such as Mary Richards of *The Mary Tyler Moore Show* or Ann Marie of *That Girl.* Working-class women tended to respond more favorably to images of women who are more affixed to their roles in the family, as opposed to either the "new" independent females or even the older images of ideal females, such as the sexpot.

11. For an excellent discussion of feminist film and television analysis, see E. Kaplan (1987:211–54).

Chapter 2

The Socio-Historical Context of *thirtysomething*

The demographic group whose lives *thirtysomething* strives to represent is historically unique, in that it came of age during the aftermath of the social and political upheavals of the 1960s and 1970s. For female viewers in or around their thirties, these upheavals were bracketed by women's large-scale entry into the labor force, beginning in the mid-1960s, and the women's movement of the late 1960s and 1970s. *Thirtysomething* invokes this historical legacy in many direct and subtle ways, through its portrayal of the day-to-day conflicts of the characters on the show.

The women on the show, for example, frequently struggle with the conflicting demands of work and family, a struggle rooted in the historical reality of shifting gender roles, and expressed in the female characters' continued angst about their own life choices and their relations to men. The characters who are single women in their thirties, like unprecedented numbers of their counterparts in the audience, have entered the work force successfully, but have not been able to achieve the more traditionally defined female goals of marriage and motherhood. The single women's predicament is reflected in a "fantasy" sequence in which the character of Ellyn Warren, who is single, appears as a guest on the talk-show *Geraldo*, speaking on the topic "Single Women Over Thirty . . . Who are they? Where do they come from? What do their friends and family think? Let's explore how this phenomenon has penetrated our society" (Gordon 1991:228). This fantasy vignette plays into and expresses not only Ellyn's frustrations with being unable to find an available man who is not threatened by her active career but, more revealingly, her anger that her friends and family seem to stand in judgment of her single status. As she reveals in another segment, she does not mind being alone in itself, as much as the feeling that other people are pitying her and making her feel like a "loser" because she does not have a mate.

The married female characters are also shown struggling with the legacy of economic and social changes in women's position as they negotiate their desires to work full time and to be home with their children. In trying to appeal to their boomer audience, then, the creators of *thirtysomething* use the boomers' unique historical location as a context for their show. And, in fact, much of the appeal of the show lies in its ability to show just how difficult it is for baby boomers, particularly women, to negotiate their gender roles in the wake of these massive historical changes. Not only does *thirtysomething* use recent historical events as a context for its characters' personal lives, but it also reproduces recent debates in the larger culture over what roles women might want to occupy.

The target audience is historically unique, therefore, but just as important, *thirtysomething* itself is unique in the way it invokes history—specifically, the history of women of this generation who find that they have been raised with seemingly conflicting goals. In this chapter I trace the way *thirtysomething* draws on the historical situation of baby-boomer women. First, I will briefly explore some of the historical transformations of American women's social roles that have occurred in the past thirty years. I will look at some of the original feminist arguments concerning the need to transform women's gender roles, as well as the ways in which women's entry into the labor force has in fact altered these roles. From there, I will outline some of the academic debates that have arisen and the ways in which *thirtysomething* invokes these debates in portraying the female characters on the program.

The Women's Movement: Background and Goals

Women's place in American society has undergone gradual yet radical transformations since at least the 1890s.[1] Female employment outside the home has been steadily increasing since that time, accompanied by a rise in the age in which women marry, a decline in the size of the average family, and a rise in the divorce rate. The only exceptions to these historical trends occurred during the 1950s, when in the aftermath of World War II a return to motherhood and childbearing became a virtual national obsession. Statistics tend to bear out this reversal, in that there appeared to be a return to earlier marriages and larger families, and a stabilization of the divorce rate (Gerson 1985:4-5). As Cynthia Fuchs Epstein notes, however, by 1984 nearly 70 percent of women aged twenty-five to fifty-four, or four out of five women workers, were employed full time. As she concludes, furthermore, by 1984 most children had a working mother; half of all mothers with children under three years of age were working, as well as 60 percent of mothers whose children were three to five, and fully 70 percent of mothers whose children were between six and thirteen (Epstein 1988:202).

Even during the 1950s, women's participation in the labor force continued to climb, although this fact was underplayed at the time. Margaret Anderson (1988) contends that by entering the labor force during the 1950s, women were able to broaden their horizons at the same time they became aware of discrimination against them in the workplace itself (see Anderson 1988:287-317). In some sense, we can begin to understand the women's movement of the 1960s and 1970s as a reaction to the contradictions that women in the 1950s experienced between the cultural ideals set out for them as happy homemakers and the realities they lived as second-class citizens entering the labor force in increasing numbers (Wallis 1989:82). The women's movement, as a social movement, arose as a political response to these contradictions. Professional women began to work within American political institutions to fight for changes in women's status. In 1961, John F. Kennedy formed a Presidential Commission chaired by Eleanor Roosevelt to document "prejudices and outmoded customs that act as barriers to the full realization of women's basic rights" (cited in Anderson 1988:293). The same year that the findings of this commission were published (1963), another pivotal work that inspired millions of women was also published, Betty Friedan's *The Feminine Mystique.* Friedan's work was an exhortation to millions of middle-class women who had received college educations but who were not working outside the home. The combination of advanced degrees with being confined to the home created an unstable situation for millions of women, which Friedan predicted would lead to mass neurosis if not rectified.

Although this cohort of white, middle-class women began to question their roles in American society in the late 1950s and early 1960s, then, and government and business began seeking to address their unequal status in the workplace, it remained for the great social upheavals of the 1960s to truly galvanize the women's movement into a full-fledged force for social change. Women who were active in the civil rights movement and the protest against the Vietnam War learned that, even as they fought for the rights of others, their own rights were being denied by the very people and organizations to whom they lent their assistance. Their second-class status in these movements, combined with the general turbulence of the 1960s, which called into question the fundamental social and political inequalities that different social groups in America faced, created the framework for women's own burgeoning consciousness and radicalization.

Many of these women came to believe that American society was characterized by fundamental social, economic, and political inequalities between the sexes. Feminists argued that it was necessary to effect changes in the primary institutions that produced and reinforced inequality for women, including the legal system, the political system, educational institutions, and, perhaps most importantly, the institution of the family.

Elaborating a critical theory of the family, they argued that the family has functioned since at least the industrial era as an important foundation of creating inequalitites between the sexes, in that it bifurcates male and female labor. Men's labor is transformed into wage labor outside the home (in factories and offices), while women are confined to unpaid labor (including the care and feeding of the young, old, and infirm) within the home. From this structural division within the nuclear family comes the ideological delineation of "separate spheres" for men and women, with different personality traits accruing to each sphere. Women, for example, are expected to be warm, caring, nurturant, and attentive to the needs of others within the nuclear family; men, on the other hand, are expected to be tough, resiliant, realistic, cunning, and aggressive, in order to survive in the wage-labor market. The inequality created by the nuclear family's division into male and female roles continues to exist today, as women go out into the paid labor force to jobs with lower pay. So-called "pink-collar jobs" for women are routinely lower-paying, as the legacy of the industrial era remains with its ideology of a primary male "family wage" and a "supplemental" female wage.

More generally, this understanding of the nuclear family as creating unequal gender roles diverged from earlier sociological readings that theorized the family as a harmonious social unit whose sexual division of labor helped to maintain a smoothly running social system. The influential sociologist Talcott Parsons's (1955) decidedly upbeat version of the family's social function, for example, stressed the necessity of having sex-role allocation in an industrialized society, without taking into account how this "allocation" creates a two-tiered system with women at the bottom. In his now-famous schema of the optimum division of labor between the sexes, Parsons argued that society benefited when women are assigned the "expressive" roles in the family as caretakers and nurturers, and husbands take on the "instrumental" role of economic supporter, because this allocation helps to maintain a stable and smooth-functioning social system in which each sex is called on to fulfill a socially necessary task, and there will not be so much role confusion that certain tasks may end up not getting done. Because theorists like

Parsons viewed sex-role differentiation as functionally necessary to secure social roles, they overlooked the ways it enforced inequality between the men and women (Parsons and Bales 1955:3–9).

Implicit in the functionalist model is the idea that the family, to use Christopher Lasch's (1977) term, is a "haven" in a heartless world, and its primary role is to offer a kind of free zone of emotion and intimacy from the harsh competitive demands of the "outside" world. Women's role within this sphere is to provide the emotional warmth, caring and nurturance that is denied individuals (men) in the dog-eat-dog world of the modern capitalist workplace. Inequalities do not exist within the family according to this model because, unlike the world "out there," there are thought to be no power relations at all in the family. Instead there is presumed to be a harmony of interests wherein the man fulfills the economic and the woman the emotional needs of the unit.

Countering this image of the family as a "haven in a heartless world," feminist social critics have argued that the family does not exist somehow outside society, but is rather itself a key area within society where gender inequalities are first produced and later played out (Baca Zinn and Eitzen 1990:129). Ultimately, feminists attacked functionalist models of the family because they felt these models ignored the ways in which the division of public and private spheres, and men's and women's roles within these spheres, contributed to women's oppression. For, even if women held to their part of the bargain and played out the expressive role of wife and mother, by the late 1950s and early 1960s many men were often themselves no longer willing to bear the primary burden of breadwinner and began to leave their families without economic support. This "flight from commitment" on the part of the male breadwinner to keep up his part of the bargain, as Barbara Ehrenreich has noted, resulted in millions of women being left on their own with young children to take care of but with very few economic resources of their own to draw on, precisely because of the societal assumption that women's paid labor was only supplemental to a male "family wage." When the male goes away, however, the woman must act as the primary breadwinner, and thus the "feminization of poverty" arises as this male wage disappears from the lives of the women and children whose survival depends on it (Ehrenreich 1984).

In launching a critique of the family, then, feminists hoped to challenge the traditional gender roles that were formed within the family and that in turn were key to maintaining the system of economic inequality in American society. While feminists have long been caricatured as seeking to destroy the family, it was always oppressive gender divisions, rather than the family itself, that was the target of their critique. One of the goals for which many feminists fought was to create a society in which both men and women could consciously and deliberately choose which roles, both inside and outside the family, they would adopt, free of societal expectations, pressures, and definitions based solely on the criterion of their biological sex.

Women, Work, and Family: Present-Day Realities and Conflicts

There have been profound changes in the lives of middle-class men and women since the early 1960s. Primary among them has been women's massive entry into the labor force due in large part to structural changes in the economy that have increased traditionally "female" jobs in the labor force, especially those in the so-called "service" professions of clerical work, health care, teaching, and sales. Women's employment has not always been by choice, however, as the discussion of the flight of the male breadwinner underscores. Even for families that stay intact and that retain the male breadwinner, the movement from a manufacturing to a service-based economy has meant the loss of hundreds of thousands of formerly secure blue- and white-collar jobs, and the chronic underemployment of a large group of formerly secure male wage-earners. In addition, real income has fallen for over twenty years. Thus women have entered the labor force in order to keep the family afloat in a troubled economy and to try to maintain a standard of living that was once a possibility with one income. Women's gains in terms of entry into the workforce must be read therefore within the context of worsening economic conditions, which force many of them to go to work from necessity (Ehrenreich and Piven 1984).

The women's movement both grew out of and nourished women's entry into the labor force as many dedicated feminists encouraged women to explore opportunities outside the home and to develop themselves in ways independent of the roles of wife and mother. By the 1980s, one of the most important messages of the women's movement—that women ought to feel free to seek personal fulfillment in the world of work as well as in their traditional roles in the family—had been absorbed into the popular consciousness.

What has been the impact of the entry of these middle-class women into the labor force on their status in society and in the family? The greatest consequence of this increased labor force participation has been their economic gains. As Heidi Hartmann (1987) points out, women are earning more money and are probably more independent from men as a result of their labor power (Hartmann 1987:45; cited in Baca Zinn and Eitzen 1990:180). Although women have undeniably made significant economic gains, these gains have not been attended by a significant transformation in their economic status (Langston 1988:128–41). Women are still fighting for equal pay for equal work, and the wage gap remains such that women make approximately 66 cents to the dollar that a man earns (Wallis 1989:85). Part of the reason for the continuing wage gap between men and women is that women remain stuck in low paying pink-collar and service sector jobs, which pay less than traditionally male-occupied jobs. This is due, in turn, to the continuing perception that women enter the workforce only in order to supplement their husbands' wages.[2]

Most women, like most men, work for the money. In a survey by the *New York Times,* fully 60 percent of women said they chose to work in order to support themselves or their families, 27 percent for extra money, and only 9 percent as a means of doing something interesting (Cowan 1989:A14).

Transforming Gender Roles: The Double Burden of Work and Family

Middle-class women's entry into the labor force has helped transform the patterns of American family life, especially for parents with young children. Whereas in 1950 approximately one out of eight women with a child under six was working, by 1984 that number had jumped to more than one of every two such women (Epstein 1988:202). But how much have women's traditional gender roles been altered by these changes? Although women have entered the workforce in dramatic numbers, they are still expected to fulfill roles at home; the burden of house and child care remains on their shoulders. As Joseph Pleck (1977) has pointed out in his discussion of the work-family role system, although both fathers and mothers are now in the labor force, it is still assumed that it is the woman, for example, who will take off from work if the child is sick. Husbands, on the other hand, are still expected to adjust their family life so that their jobs can still come first (Pleck 1977:417–27). Sociologist Arlie Hochschild has aptly described contemporary women's burden of the "second shift" the household work that women routinely perform after (and often before) a full working day.

Hochschild found that even the most "liberal" and enlightened men rarely made a dent in this labor even if they and their wives, for the sake of family peace, perceived that they did. As Hochschild notes, "Men are trying to have it both ways . . . They're trying to have their wives' salaries and still have the traditional roles at home" (1989; cited in Wallis 1989:86).

Not only individual men but society at large has been slow to respond to women's entry into the paid workforce. Employers, legislators, and government agencies have done little to execute "family friendly" policies, such as daycare or flextime, which would ease working women's burdens. This general failure to acknowledge women's two roles as wage-earners and as traditional housewives and mothers helps account for women's contemporary complaint that they have little or no time for themselves (Cowan 1989:A14).

The very persistence of patterns such as the "second shift" suggests that women may have evolved less personal assertiveness in their marriage roles than is commonly believed. Hochschild found that women who were frustrated by having to perform a second shift might try repeatedly to cajole their spouses into helping, only to end up even more angry and frustrated by virtue of the resulting marital strife. Husbands and wives who would supposedly share cooking chores, for example, would find that the husbands would forget to purchase the food in order to cook it and would end up ordering in on their night to cook. Women, on the other hand, routinely engaged in the mental labor of remembering which items of food to buy, as well as taking the time and effort and doing the manual labor of cooking it.

Many women ended up by putting up with the unequal situation in order to preserve their marriage, which they feared might fail if they tried to assert their needs for sharing the housework. These women, like so many before them, had "gone underground" with their needs. Thus women give up asking men to assume what have historically been female tasks, even though they now share the breadwinner role. They choose to accept a situation they find frustrating and exhausting, rather than persist in the struggle for household change. This makes sense if women feel that the alternative to this continued passivity is divorcing or being divorced by their husbands: given a choice between acceptance and divorce (with its attendant loss of needed income), many women are willing to accept an unequal situation.

Thus, while some changes have been made (women may ask for help), traditional roles still persist and women resign themselves to frustration. The new sexual division of family labor means that married as well as single women assume the double burden of juggling work and family responsibilities; receiving lower wages and finding subtle discrimination at work; being discouraged from acting assertive for fear of scaring away men; and not finding enough social alternatives to alleviate their burden as primary caretakers for their children. In response to a *New York Times* poll the vast majority of women of all races and economic strata agreed that the goals of the women's movement had not been fully realized and that their primary concerns today relate to work and childcare, to who takes care of the children as well as who does the majority of the housework (Belkin 1989:1, 26).

Despite the persistence of certain aspects of traditional gender roles, the world certainly does look vastly different to women today than it did to their mothers. These women have routinely begun to ask themselves a host of questions that their mothers only faintly articulated: Who am I? What do I want from life? What is most important to me? Where can I derive my feelings of self-worth? In trying to answer these questions, however, women now find themselves in a situation that more often than not demands their entry into the paid workforce even while it holds out to them the earlier cultural ideal of being the cornerstone of the family. The men in their lives are strangely silent and indeed left out of this contemporary struggle, as the culture tends to define the problems and issues as "women's problems": whether to stay home or go out and work, whether to assert oneself or act "feminine," whether to redefine oneself according to male images of success or try instead to approximate the more traditional female gender roles played out in earlier generations.

Some early feminists may have erred in proposing an over-radical solution to the problem of women's inequality, namely the dissolution of all gender roles and the nuclear family. For it is clear that even the most harried working mothers may still enjoy some tasks associated with traditional female roles, including staying home for the early years of their children's lives; what they urgently need, however, is assistance and flexibility in sharing these roles with their partners or outside caregivers. Instead of flexibility, however, many women find themselves in the bind of assuming roles and behaviors that the culture defines as conflicting or at least competing. They are encouraged to work at the same time it is assumed that they will still be the primary caregivers for home and family; defining oneself outside of one's relationship to a man is cheerfully advocated at the same time women are still made to feel less than whole without a man or a child. Thus, despite their gains, women are still trying to conform to earlier culturally defined scripts about appropriate female behavior and roles while they assume new roles and behaviors.

Feminism and Beyond: An Era of Retrenchment?

Some authors who were writing about women's issues in the late 1980s tended to echo the assessment that women have difficulty balancing competing cultural scripts. These writers were divided into different camps when it came to assigning blame. Books such as Betty Friedan's *The Second Stage* (1981) and Sylvia Hewlett's *A Lesser Life: The Myth of Women's Liberation in America* (1986) attribute women's difficulties finding men and having a family life to the women's movement's overemphasis on the pursuit of careers outside the home.

In *A Lesser Life* Hewlett levels the charge that American feminists, in calling for equal opportunities for women at work, in effect cheated large numbers of women out of a fulfilling family life, by advocating that women could enter the world of work in the same way as men; that is, that they should devote as much energy to their jobs as men had in the past. This supposed acceptance of a "male" model of work, combined with the active fight for women's reproductive rights, leads Hewlett to conclude that feminists ignored the needs of women with children or women who wanted to have children.

Echoing this critique of feminism as somehow adopting a male model of success to the exclusion of more traditionally feminine goals is Betty Friedan's aptly titled *The Second Stage.* In this work, Friedan too offers a kind of self-critique of the earlier mistakes of the "first stage" of feminism, wherein feminists launched a full-scale attack on men and the family as agents of women's oppression in order to free women from oppressive gender-role dichotomies. Friedan believes that this position, while perhaps initially necessary to eradicate the "feminine mystique" that served as a barrier to women's achievement of equality, has now been replaced by an equally pernicious "femin*ist* mystique" that tends to ignore altogether women's needs for family as it focuses primarily on women and work.

In general, this kind of writing is characterized by a re-valorization of motherhood as intrinsically satisfying and a worthwhile goal in itself. The criticism against feminism is that, in "buying into" the male models of achievement, women actually lost sight of the really important human activities of caring for one's young, activities that presumably many men would want to partake in in a more humane world (Ruddick 1982:91).

During this period of the late 1980s, other voices emerged that defended the important gains women had achieved in the previous thirty years, including expanded job opportunities and the opening up of women's roles so that they do not have to be full-time wives and mothers. For example, Kathleen Gerson, in her study of working women, *Hard Choices: How Women Decide About Work, Career, and Motherhood* (1985), points out that women of all social classes have rising work aspirations as well as ambivalence over being home full time. Many women, in other words, are grateful that they are not forced, through traditional gender role restrictions, to stay home if they do not want to, and value the fact that opportunities exist for them outside the home. The "hard choices" these women have to make relate to the daily decisions they are confronted with: between jeopardizing their jobs if they stay home with a sick child, for example, and cutting corners with their family if they give work a higher priority.

Some writers focus on the need to transform men's roles in society, citing men's failure to adopt new roles as the primary reason why women remain stuck with multiple conflicting burdens. For example, Ellen Goodman has observed that, in the so-called war between the stay-at-home mothers and working mothers, men are being totally left out of the debate. She believes that as long as the discussion is only centered around women, they will remain stuck (Goodman 1990:A7). For if women spend all their time trying to find solutions individually, rather than thinking about their problems as joint problems to be shared with their spouses, then they will inevitably find themselves solely responsible for coming up with a workable solution.

Not surprisingly, these debates about where to put the blame for women's unequal burdens are not confined to the academy, but have arisen in popular culture as well. In the popular literature of women's magazines during the late 1980s, debates continued over the legacy of the women's movement and whether its goals are still viable and worthy of women's support. In the early 1980s, articles in women's magazines tended to focus on the phenomenon of the "superwoman" who was able to do it all, and therefore have it all—a home, a family, an exciting career, and a satisfying sex life. More recent writing in women's magazines tends to focus on the financial and emotional costs of juggling competing roles. Terms such as "new woman," "mommy track," "new traditionalists," and "second shift" have come into use to describe baby-boomer women's varying attempts to answer the demands of home and family as well as careers outside the home. Media researcher Delia Conte, who did a large-scale study (1990) of women's magazines during this period, discovered that much of the writing in women's magazines centered on a high-pitched rhetorical battle between the stay-at-home mother and the working mother. Each side in the "mommy wars" lobbed criticisms at the other for being an inferior parent, ostensibly leaving each kind of mother feeling victimized by other women for her choice of staying at home or going out to work.[3]

More generally, popular literatures seemed to reflect a widespread re-evaluation of *both* men's and women's social roles as a consequence of the women's movement and women's entry into the labor force. The men's movement, for example, arose during this period as a direct response to male anxieties about men's place in the American family and their sense of role confusion over whether to adopt more female traits or retain their earlier "masculine" identities.

Thirtysomething's Treatment of Women's Changing Roles

It is against this socio-historical backdrop of the changes brought on in the wake of the women's movement and women's entry into the labor force that the creators of *thirtysomething* entered into the cultural discourse of the late 1980s and, I believe, took a fairly specific position regarding gender roles. The show explicitly or implicitly invokes women's conflicts: over work versus family; over relations between the sexes; over their own changing self-definitions; and, finally, over wanting to be free of societal expectations versus desiring to play them out. By making the portrayal of gender issues a key dramatic foil, *thirtysomething* also took up a specific position in contemporary debates, a position that offers both a re-valorization of more traditional roles for women and a critique of feminism for ignoring women's desires to inhabit more fully their roles as mothers.

For example, a key narrative strategy of *thirtysomething* is to mine the ambivalence and nostalgia that its characters feel for the ideals of the 1960s. The characters' central existential predicament is the paradox of having to accept "adult" responsibilities and roles when one was formed during a period that radically questioned these roles and duties. For male as well as female characters, each step taken toward the building of successful middle-class family life is accompanied by the consciousness of a failure to "change the world." Since one of the ways this generation tried to change the world was by opening up the gender roles available to men and women, choices surrounding work and family are freighted with this tension as well. *Thirtysomething* enacts these tensions, as we will see, by dividing up the possible roles for baby-boomer women among its female characters: single women, married women; career women, stay-at-home mothers. These roles, in turn, are portrayed as being mutually exclusive. Much of the dramatic tension of the show arises from the characters' recognition of certain consequences of roles they have already chosen and the occasional effort to change these decisions.

Although *thirtysomething* portrays a number of different life choices available to baby-boomer women, it ultimately endorses one specific choice over others, at least for the married women on the show. Although many of the ideals of the 1960s were meaningful and important, the married characters, in their attempt to be "mature" and "realistic" instead try to approximate the gender roles of their parents' generation. Hope and Michael Steadman, for example, seemingly have the most desirable and "together" life, despite their difficulties. Hope and Michael, in turn, offer the closest approximation to the traditional nuclear family of previous generations in that Hope chooses to be a full-time mother while Michael works full time outside the home. Thus, while a variety of lifestyles are portrayed, it is okay for these people to want the same things that their parents wanted.

In fact, by virtue of the way other characters are laid out—along a kind of spectrum of dysfunctioning—*not* approximating traditional roles means being stuck somehow at a more or less adolescent stage of development. For example, the character Gary is routinely shown as immature and marginal because he refuses to look for a more secure position than that of a professor at a local college. His immaturity is further underscored by his refusal to marry the woman with whom he is living and having a baby. Somehow, because of his low pay and lack of a marriage certificate, he and his partner are shown as living on the edge, not having enough money to care for their child when she falls ill. They have to run to Michael and Hope, who can supply them with money, food, and consolation because they have done the right thing by getting married and having Michael "sell out" and take a higher paying job.

In yet another example, the single character Melissa is shown as developmentally delayed in her masochistic devotion to her mother when her mother breaks her leg and needs assistance. The excessive attention that she gives her sick mother is in turn somehow related to her ambivalence about succeeding as an (adult) photographer. In addition, she feels that her mother is disappointed in her because she is not married with a family, and thus her solicitous care for her mother is a kind of compensatory act for not pleasing her in other ways. Although the mother tells Melissa at the end of the episode that she is proud of her work as a photographer and she herself does not think she would have advocated her own life as a housewife as a desirable one for her, the viewer is left with the suspicion that Melissa's devotion to her mother is a result of her inability to build a stable life for herself with her own family to take care of. Thus being single on *thirtysomething* signifies an arrested stage of development, both psychologically as well as socially.

If *thirtysomething*'s character typology presents members of more or less traditional nuclear families as more 'normal' than others, it does not show them to be necessarily more happy or mentally healthy. The nuclear family and the traditional gender roles within it are portrayed as under tremendous economic and social pressures, pressures that were not present during the seemingly halcyon days of the 1950s in which their parents raised families. Thus the memory that the thirtysomethings have of a stable, nuclear family is difficult to emulate, even if they want to (J. Rosen 1989).

The underlying message that tends to pervade *thirtysomething*, however, is that, whatever else women choose to do with their lives, the domestic front itself will never be secure unless they also firmly maintain their place as the emotional center of this sphere. Of course the world is not the same as it once was, and by implication traditional gender roles can no longer be as rigidly enforced, but the hidden hope is nevertheless for a return to a safe and secure domestic sphere where earlier gender roles prevailed. The world of *thirtysomething* thus invokes a nostalgic desire to return to an earlier, simpler life like that depicted in Frank Capra's *It's a Wonderful Life*, and in fact the production company for *thirtysomething* was given the same name as the town depicted in the film. The predicament of the protaganist for *thirtysomething*'s dramatic terrain may be seen as borrowed from that of the main character in the film as well. Driven to despair by economic and family pressures, George, the main character, takes an extended trip into an otherworld (his psyche) with his conscience (Angel Clarence) in order to discover the value of his small, daily acts against the larger claims of history, war, and culture. Like George, the main character of *thirtysomething*, Michael Steadman, must daily do battle with his inner psyche to discover the 'really' important things in his life, namely, his wife, Hope, and his daughter, Janey. More generally, nostalgia for earlier, seemingly more peaceful periods will emerge as a guiding theme on the show as a coveted, if unrealistic, resolution to the crises that are brought on in the wake of changing gender roles.

In terms of content, many of the show's themes concern the loneliness of women who remain single and forestall childbearing, or the compromises made by married women who try to work full time and raise children. The formal means through which these ideologies are articulated are specific techniques of rendering the interior life of the characters on the show. Through fantasy, flashback, and interior monologue, *thirtysomething* brings a heightened psychological realism to the development of characters. It is by constructing and identifying with *thirtysomething*'s characters—the four primary female characters in particular—that women come to internalize, in their own specific ways, the show's ideologies about gender. And while all the characters display their ambivalence about their lives, the characters who most resemble the new traditionalist of pop mythology are portrayed as having the most viable lives. In this way, *thirtysomething* implicitly valorizes women who want to do the same things with their life. It may be helpful to describe the four main female characters on *thirtysomething* at this point in order to elaborate upon the ways in which prevailing stereotypes of women were constructed in popular culture during this period.

Hope Steadman: The New Traditionalist

In the late 1980s, in magazines from *Esquire* to *Ladies Home Journal*, the "new traditionalist" was touted as a new model for women. These were the women who actively chose to re-create earlier social roles for women, which had presumably been radically questioned during the women's movement, but which now seemed to be a new alternative for women who have wearied of the rigors of combining work and family. The trouble was, she looked suspiciously like the old model of stay at home wife and mother; the twist was that these women had active careers in the past, but have now chosen, at least temporarily, to embrace the roles of wife and mother. Hope Steadman was the new traditionalist of popular media folklore brought to life.

Thirtysomething is nothing if not sophisticated, and although it places Hope in this role on the show, we view her questioning it periodically. Far from being the Mom of the 1950s, Hope is well aware that full-time motherhood is a decision, and in fact she frequently questions this role. In this way, *thirtysomething* takes the stereotype of the new traditionalist and gives it depth, precisely by exploring the emotional tensions involved in forgoing work and making the decision to be a full-time wife and mother.

Whereas the new traditionalist of magazine ads was confident and unapologetic, Hope can be full of anxiety, boredom, and self-doubt. Hope is situated squarely in the realm of family, not of work. Educated, intelligent, and pretty, she has a new baby when the show opens, and she is shown trying to grapple with what this new role means for her after having attended an elite Ivy League school and having begun an exciting career as a researcher for a magazine. During many episodes, Hope questions her decision to stay at home, as when she makes periodic forays back into the world of work, but finds that the demands of even part-time jobs or volunteer work conflict with her jobs at home, doing childcare and taking care of the house. In one episode, for example, Hope is offered work in Washington, DC, which would require the whole family to move. As we will see, this job offer is complicated by the fact not only that she is eight and a half months pregnant, but that the person who offers her the job is also in love with her. In a second episode, as will also be shown, Hope wrestles between the decision to go back to work and have a career versus having a second child. In both cases, Hope expresses outright her dissatisfaction and boredom with being home full time, yet in both cases, when the real or imagined demands of the prospective work conflict with her roles at home, she inevitably opts out of the paid labor force and back into the domestic sphere.

In other episodes, on the other hand, Hope expresses guilt over her decision to stay home, not because she is unhappy about it but rather precisely because it gives her such joy. She feels torn up that her friends, especially her single female friends, will somehow stand in judgment of her, because they cannot understand what powerful feelings she has toward her child and her need to be with the baby full time. Just as the single women on the program feel pressure from their married female friends to get married and have children, then, so too do the married women feel pressure from their single friends that they have somehow given up on life by leaving the paid labor force. Much of the guilt and anxiety Hope feels thus relates to her sense that she should not be enjoying the role of full-time mother so much, because others will think she has "lost it" in pablum and forgotten who the "real" Hope is.

Ironically enough, in various magazine articles that appeared at the time, the actress who plays Hope, Mel Harris, was often portrayed as happily combining the roles of mother, wife, and career woman. In a *Redbook* magazine article of May 1991, for example, entitled "Motherhood Is Even Sweeter the Second Time Around," Harris is shown cheerfully holding her one-year-old while looking every bit the glamorous Hollywood star. Describing her trailer or dressing room for the series as a "home away from home," Harris attributes her ability to juggle a grueling work schedule of days that go from six in the morning until eight at night to her husband, Cotter Smith, who also was starring in his own series at the time, *Equal Justice* ("Motherhood Is Even Sweeter the Second Time Around" 1991:26). Describing her responsibility to raise her two children as a joint one that she shares with her husband, the article also mentions that she has a full-time nanny to help as well. On *thirtysomething*, however, Mel Harris's character seems to have a lot more difficulty combining the rigors of parenting and work in the paid labor force, as she decides to forgo a career to raise her children.

Although Hope thus expresses a great deal of ambivalence about adopting the role of wife and mother wholesale, at the same time a large part of her wants to be able to devote herself to being a wife and mother full time, which would not be possible if she went back to work. This, then, is Hope's conflict: how to mediate between the pull to have a career, and the presumably equally strong pull to inhabit the traditional role of full-time wife and mother.

Nancy: The Old Traditionalist

Hope's best friend Nancy is also a full-time wife and mother. Unlike Hope, however, Nancy never made an active choice to become a full-time wife and mother; rather, these were roles she found herself in, even though she had also wanted to pursue a career as an artist. Nancy often finds herself thinking about her life choices, which replicate the traditional model for women, and subsequently asking herself, "Where am I?" Thus, despite their differences, Hope and Nancy are on the same side of an ideological divide that *thirtysomething* posits between married mothers and single women.

In Nancy's struggles, viewers are able to witness the transition from the "old" to the "new" model of women most clearly. For example, in the earlier seasons, Nancy is an unhappy housewife, putting up with a traditional bourgeois domestic arrangement that leaves her haggard, unappreciated, and coping with a husband who is absent and philandering. Her response to this situation is one of low-grade vituperativeness, silent anger, and a sort of generalized sense of resentment. This Nancy is a kind of "pre-liberation" version of the housewife who is clearly not happy with her life but does not yet have the emotional resources to make changes in that life. As one viewer said of her:

> Remember when Nancy was very unsure of herself and hadn't really found herself, she was like very insecure, she was almost uncomfortable in her own skin, she was a good mother, but other than that, she didn't really seem complete. (transcript no. 4)

Nancy begins to undergo a transformation, however, in the wake of her separation from her husband. This separation forces her to confront a number of issues in her life, including a re-evaluation of her traditional domestic arrangements, coping with being a single parent, and re-discovering her sexuality as a single woman. Her "coping mechanisms," in turn, go from a kind of silent suffering to an airing of her feelings of anger and confusion, and in this way she is shown as emerging from a pre-liberationist fog of unhappiness to a more active role of actively questioning the sources of her unhappiness.

This process is most clearly articulated in later episodes, where she is stricken with ovarian cancer. At first, the fact that of all the female characters on the show, Nancy is the one who is given ovarian cancer seems to be in keeping with earlier representations of her as a long-suffering, indeed tragic figure. It is almost as if her ovarian cancer is the logical outcome of assuming the burdens of everyone else for so long that, finally, they have grown like a cancer on her "mothering" (reproductive) organs and have to be removed. Being stricken with ovarian cancer, however, allows her to question her feelings about herself as a wife and mother, because she is afraid that in losing her reproductive organs she will no longer be the woman (mother) she once was. Although her reproductive organs are removed, Nancy nevertheless emerges from the trauma not only as more human but indeed as a character with more depth and strength than was previously accorded her. The whole cancer episode raised her stature in the eyes of many of the viewers, who interpreted her reaction to these events as evidence of her ability to be strong and cope with life events in an assertive manner.

For Nancy, then, the role she plays as long-suffering and martyred is complicated by her gradual articulation of dis-ease with wholly identifying with the traditionally passive sides of this role, and her subsequent attempts to reclaim other, more active parts of herself. Like Hope, however, Nancy represents *thirtysomething*'s attempt to reach women who, while feeling conflicted about their roles as wives and mothers, nevertheless want to play out those roles in some way.

Melissa: The Stereotype of the "Single Woman"

> Melissa is a single, freelance photographer. Not attractive. Has a problem with relationships. Feels her biological clock is running or ran out. (questionnaire no. 5)

Melissa Steadman is single and in her thirties, and has a career as a struggling photographer. She is perpetually concerned about finding "Mr. Right," and wondering whether her biological "clock" for childbearing is running out. Unlike the "gung ho" career woman represented by the character of Ellyn Warren, Melissa, despite her career, demonstrates a strong desire for more traditional female roles, including getting married and having children. In its portrayal of Melissa, *thirtysomething* implicitly drew on larger cultural discussions that were taking place in popular culture about single women during this period. These discussions were ambivalent about women who remained unmarried, emphasizing their lowly status as an object of pity while at the same time somewhat valorizing them for their independence and ability to be their own persons.

The "single woman" during this period was viewed, at least in part, as a pitiable figure, lonely and isolated and waiting for the right man to come along and save her from the sonorous roar of her biological clock. Gerri Hirshey, for example, looking at popular images of single women during this period, has linked up these negative images to the culture's re-emphasis on re-creating the nuclear family as the most desirable social arrangement (Hirshey 1989). The "single woman" was an object of fear and pity because she deviated from the newly constituted nuclear family, which had itself been questioned in the social experiments of the 1960s and 1970s but which now stood as an object of nostalgia and emulation. Put in other terms, the "single woman" represented the dark side of the boomers' search for the lost American family, serving as a constant reminder that this family is not an immutable object of nature, but must be constantly reproduced in each generation (Hirshey 1989:52).

Implicit here is the idea that the women's movement somehow jeopardized this fragile social arrangement by admonishing women to focus on other areas of their lives besides men and family. In this framework, the "single woman" stood out not only as a depressed figure but as a kind of nightmarish embodiment of a social movement that advocated independence from marriage and the family. Even the top-grossing film of 1987 seemed to convey this idea in symbolic form. As Josh Henkin observes, *Fatal Attraction* reveals these anxieties in no uncertain terms: "Even the most successful, single working women can be psychotic spinsters who will kill themselves and others to nab a man" (Henkin 1989:65).

These ideas about the depression of single women tied in with larger cultural images that portrayed women as having difficulty finding available men, as well as suffering from high degrees of infertility because they put off marriage and motherhood. A study by Harvard and Yale researchers in 1986, which was widely publicized during this period, found that if a college educated woman waited until she was thirty to get married, she had only a 20 percent chance of finding someone. These statistics plunged to 5 percent by age thirty-five and 1.3 percent by age forty. The ultimate message repeated in many publications was that it was easier to be highjacked on a plane than it was to try to get married if you were a woman over forty (Faludi 1991:3).

As Susan Faludi has pointed out, however, the reality was that, if anything, there was a woman shortage *for men* in this age group, rather than the highly touted "man shortage." The proportion of single women at this time was about one in five, a lower figure than at any time in the twentieth century except the 1950s (Faludi 1991:15). Even though the "man shortage" was a fiction produced by a culture that was trying to scare women into getting married, these messages did in fact do damage to women by making them extremely anxious that they would not be able to find a husband. Most of the women I interviewed, both single and married, knew about the results of this study, and as Faludi shows, the number of single women aged twenty-five and older who feared they would never get married went from 14 percent before the study to 39 percent one year after the study came out (Faludi 1991:18).

Although the single woman was mostly portrayed at this time as an object of pity and indeed horror, standing as both a victim of the women's movement and a perpetual outsider to the newly constituted nuclear family, at the same time she also was accorded a kind of grudging admiration. She was able to have strong friendships outside the nuclear family, particularly with other women; in addition, she was able to have an independent lifestyle, exploring and developing different sides of herself. In this way, she represented the positive aspects of the women's movement, which encouraged women to explore their identities apart from their relationships to men and children.

For example, in some of the prime-time television programs of this period—*Designing Women* and *Golden Girls*—single women were portrayed as having strong and interesting friendships with other women. *Designing Women* revolved around four women owners of an interior decorating firm, and while the humor is often related to their search for "Mr. Right," their friendships with one another offer a positive, indeed affirmative, portrait of happy, active lives as single women. *Golden Girls* was similarly structured around four women, this time widowed or divorced, who live with one another and have formed intense bonds. While much of their humor, too, consists of their attempts to find men, their friendship with each other suggests that they have found strength and happiness in one another's company.

All of this is to say that the representation of the "single woman" in recent popular cultural representations seemed much more ambiguous than an initial reading might suggest: the single woman wants a man, yet she enjoys her freedom; she craves domesticity, yet she can also have an exciting love life; she desires bondedness, yet she also has her autonomy, and so on. While portraying the loneliness and unhappiness associated with being a single woman in the 1980s and 1990s, then, these shows also contain a barely perceptible allusion to the benefits of being single.

These contradictory images are especially evident in the portrayal of Melissa on *thirtysomething*, who is shown as more independent and creative and as having stronger friendships with people outside a monogamous, man-woman relationship than the other characters on the show are allowed to have. In this way, *thirtysomething* offered a kind of double image; namely, that being single is both lonely and exhilarating, isolating and conducive to making different kinds of friendships. And, as will be shown later on in our discussion of viewer responses to the show, it is perhaps for this reason that Melissa generated contradictory reactions from viewers, depending on whether they felt positively or negatively, or both, about being single.

Ellyn: The Stereotype of the "Career Woman" as Gargoyle

> [Ellyn] is a typical career woman, but deep down I think she was jealous of Hope. (questionnaire no. 2)

Of all the female characters on *thirtysomething*, it is through the character of Ellyn that we witness the supposed consequences of "careerism" on women, namely, that they will somehow lose the very core of what it means to be a woman as they try to approximate a male model of achievement. For while Melissa has a career, she also desires a home and family. Ellyn, on the other hand, lacks any qualities associated in the minds of viewers with being a mature female adult, including the capacity for warmth or nurturance or the ability to bond and form human relationships with others.[4]

This dichotomization of social roles into career (male) versus human relationships (female), furthermore, explains why the "hybrid" category of "career woman," as represented by the character of Ellyn, invites such social opprobrium. For Ellyn is understood as somehow putting her career before the other areas in life that a woman is supposed to excel at, namely, the "business" of caring for other human beings. This hostility to Ellyn seems based in part on larger cultural assumptions of what a "mature" femininity might consist of, assumptions that remain deeply rooted in many women's minds, despite the women's movement's attempts to open up traditional constructions of femininity.

For example, sociologist Lillian Rubin (1990) has pointed out, along with Nancy Chodorow (1978), Carol Gilligan (1982), and others, that most women are still socialized to become wives and mothers and to direct their lives toward the care of others. Their identity as women is therefore tied to their capacity to form close human relationships, and their status and sense of balance in the world as mature females is based on their socialized capacity to form intimate connections with others. Men, on the other hand, are routinely socialized to form their identity through their relationship to the outside world, which is often translated into the world of work. This dichotomization of men and women explains why the character of Ellyn was construed in such a uniformly negative light, for she was viewed as being the least able to demonstrate those qualities that have been associated with what it means to be a mature female.

What is most revealing about these responses, perhaps, is that Ellyn seemed to invite disapproval to the extent that she not only refuses to behave like a mature female, that is, to say she wants to "settle down" and get married and have children, but she also ends up behaving like a man in *all* spheres of her life. For Ellyn exhibits precisely those traits that single men in our culture have often been accused of: selfishness, inability to commit in a relationship, lack of interest in settling down, and so on. Ellyn has, in a sense, gone almost off the deep end of gender roles: at the very least, her femininity was seen as somehow out of kilter and she was thought of as mentally unstable and immature. This representation of Ellyn as mentally unbalanced, in turn, is underscored on *thirtysomething* by her visits to a psychiatrist.[5] To the degree that Ellyn is portrayed as highly sexual, furthermore, this becomes part of a generalized construction of a somewhat distorted femininity. Her "sluttishness," in other words, is often portrayed as a kind of neurotic defense against trying to approximate the more acceptable goals of wife and motherhood.

Ultimately, even when Ellyn displays a hyper- or excessive femininity, it only demonstrates just how far she has veered from a "mature" femininity. This loss of balance, and consequent instability, is thus inexorably linked to her inability to establish a minimum degree of mature femininity, understood as a capacity to form close human bonds. In pursuing her career singlemindedly, Ellyn loses her claim to mature female status in the world, that is, to be a nurturer. As one woman summed it up:

> They show her [Ellyn] like being really repressed. Because a career woman can't be a nurturer. (transcript no. 10)

It is perhaps not surprising that *thirtysomething* would portray Ellyn in such grim terms, if we look at the social context that female viewers find themselves in. This social context still makes it difficult for women to achieve in the outside world and at the same time have a fulfilling home and family life. Ellyn's character may reflect a desire to explore women's hidden fears that, in deviating too far from the traditional areas of female identity, they will somehow jeopardize their chances for a successful home life. It is not, then, that women do not want to have an interesting career but that they are concerned with how they will negotiate their careers while keeping both their identities as women and their goals of having a successful home and family life.

Conclusion

One of the primary ways *thirtysomething* tries to draw women into the fictional narratives of the show is through portraying the supposedly different life choices available to women, as represented by the four primary female characters on the show. As we have seen, the female characters are often portrayed precisely in terms of their fears and conflicts over adopting one role or life choice to the exclusion of other possible roles, as when the married female characters Hope and Nancy feel like they have ruined their chance to have an active career by staying home, or when Ellyn and Melissa feel as if they will never get to make that choice and will remain without a husband or a family (Rosen 1989:30).

By dividing up the social roles available to women in terms of individual female characters, *thirtysomething* ends up reproducing popular stereotypes of different roles for women, such as the "new traditionalist" or "career woman." Ultimately it implicitly valorizes the role of the new traditionalist as the best one women can hope for, in that at least the homemaker does not have to sacrifice home and family as the career woman does. But I believe that *thirtysomething* is also successful in articulating the anxiety associated with *all* these roles, including that of the new and old traditionalists.

This presentation of the conflicts attendant on the different roles available to women, then, is what contributes to viewers' sense that *thir-*

tysomething is realistic. At the same time, however, Hope and Nancy invariably end up as the winners in the "happiness sweepstakes" of the show. Their issues and crises inevitably resolve themselves by showing them joyfully and snugly back in the bosom of the family while the single women have little solace except when they choose to match up in a union with a man (as Ellyn eventually does, in a sappy episode devoted to her marriage to a *thirtysomething* version of "Mr. Right").

More generally, the confusion and ambivalence of the female characters enacted weekly in the prime-time "morality plays" on *thirtysomething* must be viewed within the broader context of popular culture during this period. Susan Faludi, in her groundbreaking work *Backlash: The Undeclared War Against American Women* (1991), discusses how various elements of American culture and society had conspired by the late 1980s to roll back women's rights. In fact, the decade of the 1980s may be characterized by an intensive, if not necessarily concerted, effort on the part of various groups to stem the advances women were making during this period.[6] A new wave of anti-woman, especially anti-feminist, images began to appear in the areas of media, fashion, popular culture, and literature. Major news items fed the public misleading and erroneous information about the rise in the number of women who could not find husbands, the huge drop in birth rates, and the dangers of daycare. On television, images began to proliferate of women who were once again housewives or, alternatively, cold and heartless career women.[7] Even in the area of self-help literature, a common reference point for many women, women were continually being devalued, as they were blamed for being involved or "co-dependent" in relationships with men who were addicted, abusive, or prone to incest.

These anti-woman activities were not part of an orchestrated effort on the part of any one group, say the Reagan administration or the Heritage Foundation, to enlist reactionary talk-show hosts, fashion designers, and recanting feminists to agitate against women's gains. Rather, as Faludi suggestively notes, these activities functioned as a kind of "preemptive strike" on a number of fronts against the *potential* changes that might be wrought by attempts to secure equal rights for women. These reactions occurred, then, less in response to actual, concrete gains on the part of women than in response to the fear that changes were *about* to occur. The images that were put forth in popular culture are best understood, then, as efforts to conquer the hearts and minds of American men and women before changes actually take place, thereby trying to stem the tide of potential change.

Notes

1. See Tilly and Scott (1978) and Kessler-Harris (1982) for excellent discussions of women's transforming roles.

2. In fact, despite these women's entry into the workforce, women now make up 57 percent of the American poor. Writers such as Barbara Ehrenreich and Frances Fox Piven (1984) attribute women's increasing impoverishment to at least two factors. First, since men's wages often do not provide enough money for a family to survive, women have to contribute a substantial portion to the family wages. However, since women are stuck in low-paying jobs, this is not enough to raise their families out of poverty. Second, because half the marriages in the United States now end in divorce and because child-support payments are more often than not negligible, women now find themselves in the role of sole financial support for the household, but do not earn a wage that could keep them above the poverty line. What this means is that many women formerly supported by wage-earning males now have to work, whether they want to or not.

3. Commenting on this battle, Delia Conti notes that, whether they worked or not, both kinds of mothers tended to exclude their husbands from this debate. Criticizing this tendency in the rhetoric of the "mommy wars," Conti, like Goodman, concludes by challenging women to move beyond fighting one another and also to ask men to enter this debate. See Conti (1990):29.

4. The character of Ellyn draws on cultural stereotypes of the gung-ho "career woman" who, while successful in her chosen field, is a miserable failure in her personal life. Interestingly enough, the construction of Ellyn as a "ball-busting" corporate career woman (in fact, she does not even work for a corporation) is not immediately apparent, in that all the female characters, in various ways, could be said to have pursued or be currently involved in careers. Hope, for instance, had a thriving career as a researcher at one point, and is shown in different seasons making forays back into her job. Nancy, too, experiments with a career writing children's books and, in the 1990 season, teaches an art course. Susannah, a secondary character on the show, works at a non-profit social service agency. And Melissa pursues a career as a commercial photographer.

While all these women, then, can be said to have (or have had) career experience, it is interesting that Ellyn, above all the others, should be cited by the female viewers as the "career woman" on the show. When asked what it is about the character of Ellyn, other than the fact that she works very hard at her job, that led them to make this assessment, the women cited the fact that she puts her career *first.* In other words, they seemed to perceive "career women" as putting their work before other things in their lives, including human relationships.

5. What is most interesting, however, is that Ellyn is not the only character shown visiting a psychiatrist. Nancy visits a therapist with Elliot while they are having marital troubles, and Melissa is often shown in dialogue with her therapist. Yet, none of the viewers I talked to mentioned Nancy's or Melissa's visits. Ellyn's visits, on the other hand, were often cited as validation for their assessment of her character as immature, unstable, selfish, self-destructive, and so on.

6. Some examples can be seen in the federal government's decision not to enforce equal employment initiatives. In addition, the courts chose not to back women's rights rigorously, and repeatedly let anti-discrimination cases drop rather than pursue them (Faludi 1991:454). Perhaps most pernicious were the court decisions and corporate policies concerning women's rights in the workplace. In sexual harassment cases, for example, the rights of those who were harassing were commonly elevated above those of the women being harassed. Faludi cites cases as well of women who were ordered to terminate their pregnancies or lose their jobs. Other cases sought to protect the rights of fetuses to such an extent that the women who were carrying the fetuses effectively lost their rights. Abortion struggles during this period can also be read as one more example of how women's rights were being pitted (and devalued) in relation to the rights of the unborn, and the nuclear family was being reconstituted at women's expense.

7. Even the fashion industry played its part by inundating the women's wear market with Lacroix's bubble skirts, teddies, bustiers, or, alternatively, heavily padded shoulders that dwarfed women's breasts in an armor of shoulderpads (Faludi 1991:454).

Chapter 3

The Stories of *thirtysomething*

As we have seen, the creators of *thirtysomething* attempted to portray the personal conflicts of their audience as a means of drawing them into the program. Marshall Herskovitz and Edward Zwick, the show's creators, who had worked together off and on in film and television since the early 1980s, often described their original motive for making the show as a desire to represent the ordinary, everyday lives of people like themselves, that is, white, urban, upper middle-class married people in their thirties with young children (Lantos 1987:50).

Although *thirtysomething* ultimately fell victim to changing strategies in network marketing, for the four-year period in which it ran, it was innovative in its portrayal of the oppositional tensions or "dialectic" of the thirtysomething generation. One way to understand this dialectic lies in the tension between wanting to be free from tradition while at the same time wanting the stability and coherence that tradition seemed to have brought earlier generations. This is the familiar predicament of all moderns, brought up to date in the 1980s for a particular class. For example, in the first episode we will explore, Michael re-examines his atheism in the wake of a car accident involving his wife, Hope. The shock of his wife's accident eventually leads him back to temple at the close of the episode, as he reconciles his earlier questioning of religion with an acceptance that he wants some kind of connection to his Jewish roots. The dialectic exists for Hope, too, although hers is not a religious questioning so much as a radical break that she experiences between her desire to live out her earlier role as a Princeton graduate and "overachiever" with her equally strong pull to play out the role of stay-at-home wife and mother. The stories of *thirtysomething* thus play out the familiar dialectic of modern life and demonstrate some of the ways in which gender conflicts were portrayed for women in popular culture during this period. These representations often downplayed the socio-political problems that underlay the gender crises, namely, how to alter family and work policies to allow adequate time off when children are very young; how to shift roles at home so that men and women truly share all the domestic labor; how to re-negotiate gender roles in the area of intimacy and sexuality so that both men and women can experience autonomy and commitment to the other, and so on. Instead, these socio-political problems for men and women were transformed into "women's problems" and the lens remained tightly focused on how each woman resolved her own dilemma, apart from any larger community of women or society as a whole.

For example, in the first story we will see what the loss of women from the domestic sphere means, as expressed symbolically through Hope's car accident. At first it is unclear what strange malady has befallen Hope as a result of the car accident, but the impact of this mysterious injury is that Hope is no longer able to fulfill her primary role as caretaker. The episode is resolved, interestingly enough, with the discovery that the "illness" is in fact a pregnancy. Thus, Hope is re-inscribed into the domestic sphere through her pregnancy and her husband's return to his religious faith. For our purposes, it is instructive to note that the prospect of women leaving the home (expressed symbolically through Hope's accident) is greeted with an existential crisis on the part of the male character of such proportions that he reaches for pre-modern anchors (religion) to allay his anxiety about the fragility of his domestic universe.

In the second story, told from the point of view of both Michael and Hope, we witness how the crisis of women leaving the domestic sphere is played out when Hope tries to return to work. Through a series of vignettes we see how Michael tries to work through his complicated feelings of wanting Hope to remain at home, as expressed through his desire for her to get pregnant again. For Hope, on the other hand, the crisis is that she has already been home with the first child and wants to resume her career, rather than be tied even more to the home through having a second child. The episode is resolved when Hope decides to get pregnant again and puts aside the prospect of resuming an active career. In fact, Hope is not given any opportunities for thinking through how it might be possible to do both, either by having Michael take a more active role in the home or by thinking about outside options—for example, how the workplace might be socialized to include on-site daycare. This episode is thus instructive not only for the ways in which it defines crises for women, but more revealingly, for how it frames the solutions, which in Hope's case lie in an almost religious faith that things will somehow work out.

In the third story, we see how the problem of motherhood is framed for women on the program, through an episode that deals with the single female character of Ellyn Warren and her decision to become a kind of surrogate mother to her lover's child. Once again, we see how the worldview of *thirtysomething* tends to divide women into those who have nurturing capacities and those who do not, with women who have active careers being shown to be somehow emotionally incapable of inhabiting the role of mother. Rather than explore how *men* might become more involved in the role of parenting, or whether it might be possible to make the workplace more parent-friendly so that women might be able to inhabit both roles, the episode deals with whether Ellyn has the emotional tools to take care of another person, given her neurotic, hard-driving, "ball-busting" career woman persona.

Together, these stories represent an eloquent example of how these issues were framed for women during this period. By exploring in detail episodes that deal with the conflicts that the female characters experience over work, family, sexual intimacy, friendships, and so on, we can better understand how *thirtysomething* tried to open up these issues for its audiences and then foreclosed them with fairly conservative solutions.

Threats to the Family/Domestic Sphere, or "Michael Discovers God"

One of the themes explored in many episodes of *thirtysomething* relates to concerns about what would happen to the nuclear family if women could no longer fulfill their traditional role within it. In these episodes, the underlying fear is that, when women are no longer able to fulfill their function as the center of the domestic universe, this world is torn asunder. These issues are raised most starkly in an early episode in which Hope has a car accident.

The episode opens with all the main characters playing Trivial Pursuit, the quintessential yuppie board game of the 1980s, in front of the fire in Hope's and Michael's living room. The living room scene exists as the "before time," that is, before Hope's accident. It also symbolically makes Michael and Hope's house the emotional center of the show. The living room is shot in warm, earthy tones with gauze over the camera lens, and the ubiquitous acoustic guitar twangs gently in the background. This is the site for the "good times" on the show, and the scene is echoed by various wine commercials showing young, thirtyish couples presumably enjoying the same good life. For our purposes, it is helpful to note that this opening scene establishes a relatively stable, happy domestic sphere, where friends can relax with one another and spend their leisure time in "trivial pursuits" in front of the hearth.

In the show's opening line, Gary, the sixties holdover character who often functions as the moral conscience for the other members of the show, picks the Trivial Pursuit category of old tv shows and remarks, "Can't this generation define itself other than by theme songs from old television shows?" This line clues the audience into what will be one of the underlying themes of the episode: namely, that although most people of this generation consume tv "ironically," the categories they grew up with were nevertheless defined by these early tv shows, and many of their assumptions about what domestic life will be like can be traced back to earlier domestic situation comedies.[1]

The opening vignette thus functions as a sophisticated postmodern "show within a show" rumination on television and its cultural impact on our lives. We know we are watching a television show, and the program is commenting on earlier programs, thereby distinguishing it from other shows that lack this self-consciousness. But instead of inviting us to question television in terms of our hindsight knowledge about earlier shows, this dialogue in effect draws us into the drama by having us identify precisely with the nostalgia of the characters for these earlier programs.

The opening scene thus ends up being a wonderfully inclusionary gesture, offering the audience something we can all relate to and comforting us in the knowledge that yes, we know those earlier shows were not realistic, but parts of us still cling to those shows for the vision of the domestic world they offer. With a "hipness unto death" (Mark Miller's trenchant phrase for the ironic positioning of contemporary television watchers), we can then indulge in our fantasies of the domestic sphere as portrayed on earlier shows, all the while comfortably positioning ourselves, with the characters on *thirtysomething*, as knowing subjects of an era that has supposedly receded far into the past.

The theme of nostalgia for the domestic world of early 1960s television continues throughout the show in a series of anti-realist flashbacks that Michael has, which literally transpose him along with Hope and the rest of the characters into old episodes of the *Dick Van Dyke Show*, a domestic comedy from the early sixties. Michael's eyes wander off periodically while he is watching television, and instead of the program he is watching he sees himself and his wife on the television screen as Dick Van Dyke and Mary Tyler Moore. Everything is as it was in the earlier show, right down to the smallest detail, from the black and white screen to the hairdos, to the canned laughter and trivial sitcom situations the characters find themselves in.

For much of the show, whenever Michael experiences fear about losing Hope and by implication loss of his domestic sphere, the sitcom flashes to these early TV "family scripts" in his head. The flashbacks, one of *thirtysomething*'s more consistent anti-realist techniques, express Michael's wish to go back to a simpler time when the domestic sphere was stable and secure. What is so sophisticated about this interplay between contemporary life and the life of canned sixties sitcoms, is how the audience is made to take the point of view of Michael, who knows the sitcom is not real yet fervently desires a return to it, so much so that he literally transposes himself and his family back into it. As we will later see, this is almost exactly what many female viewers do with *thirtysomething*—that is, imaginatively use it to project and reflect on their own life conflicts.

In the next scene Hope and Michael are in the kitchen, preparing to leave for work. This is Hope's first foray back into the workworld, after having her first child and being home the child's first year. Hope is feeding Janey, and Michael is stirring the breakfast cereal at the stove. Hope is getting ready to take the baby to daycare when Janey spills her breakfast. She then yells "Michael" in frustration, although it was Janey who spilled the breakfast. She goes to clean it up, and Michael hands her a paper towel, responding to her yelling at him. The visual impact of this scene is that Hope is indeed the center of the domestic universe, a kind of whirling dervish who accomplishes a number of tasks at once as she prepares to leave the house to put in a full day's work at an office.

The conversation that takes place in this scene reinforces the idea that Hope is in charge of the home. She discusses what presents to get for whom for Christmas and Hanukkah, as well as what will be needed for the holiday dinner she is organizing. Michael is given orders by Hope, to pick up this item or that, but it is clear who is in charge of these domestic duties. Furthermore, while she may appear harried in this opening scene, doing and planning a hundred different things at once, we know that she is basically happy and cheerful in this role and is eagerly looking forward to the family dinner and the gift giving.

Michael, too, seems content with this set-up. All in all, we have a domestic vision approximating the ones of the 1960s sitcoms, and it is indeed at this point that we witness Michael's first flashback to the *Dick Van Dyke Show*. Here, the traditional gender roles are portrayed as greatly exaggerated, but we as the audience are nevertheless invited to make the same comparison Michael is obviously making between his life and the earlier sitcom's portrayals of men and women. For example, both Nancy and Hope are portrayed in these flashback episodes in hyper-domestic roles, down to wearing aprons and worrying about overflowing dishwashers. The men are shown worrying about their businesses and getting excited over new cars. The sitcom scenes, in other words, show an exaggerated version of domestic life where gender roles were clearly delineated.

Michael's and Hope's domestic tranquility is abruptly shattered, however, when Michael gets a call at his office informing him that Hope has been in a car accident and that her condition is as yet unknown. It turns out that she is not seriously injured and the baby who was with her in the car is also fine. Throughout the rest of the episode, however, Hope is shown at home convalescing, and she is given to strange, inexplicable bouts of dizziness that convince Michael, the supposedly neurotic Jewish character, that she indeed has something seriously wrong with her.

Hope's illness calls into question her ability to fulfill her roles as wife and mother; this inability in turn gives rise to the real fear underlying the episode: namely, that when women are unable to fulfill their traditional gender roles, the domestic universe itself is threatened. The fact that women's illnesses represent threats to the domestic sphere itself reinforces the cultural attitude that women are the primary caretakers of this sphere, even if both spouses work. For women, whether they work inside the home or out, illness represents not economic dissolution but dissolution of the domestic sphere, precisely because it is assumed that they are the ones keeping that sphere together in the first place.

After Hope's accident, Michael insists on taking care of the holiday chores; the implication is that these chores were assumed to be Hope's job. Though he offers to help out, we see him balking at having to get so many gifts for so many different people (he instead suggests just making a donation to charity) and he further questions why they have to have a holiday dinner at all. The message is thus that, were it not for Hope, Michael would not bother with these domestic holiday activities.

In another scene, when Michael arrives while Hope is out shopping after the accident, he becomes frantic that she has gotten into another car accident. We see him searching furiously through the rooms of the house and finding them in complete disarray. Hope's absence is represented by the unmade bed, the unwashed dishes, and the toys on the floor of the baby's room. When it turns out that Hope just went to get cranberry sauce, Michael's fear turns into anger. The implicit message behind this scene is twofold: Hope's absence represents domestic chaos, a literal and figurative mess; and Hope is so intent on reclaiming her domestic role that she would recklessly brave an impending snowstorm to get a trivial food item from the grocery store. Hope defends herself by saying that, if she does not resume taking care of her holiday chores, she will be too afraid ever to go out again. The implication is that, in order to feel like her old self again, that is, her old domestic self, she must resume her mantle as the primary household organizer.

This theme of the family's need for a wife and mother to fulfill more traditional gender roles as a way to ward off the threats to their domestic universe is taken further in the episode's conclusion. When Hope returns with the cranberry sauce and is castigated by Michael, she informs him that the reason she has been fainting is not because of some internal injury caused by the accident, but rather because she is pregnant. Tears of fear dissolve into tears of joy at the realization that everything is okay—okay in a real sense and not in a sitcom sense, as Hope joyfully reclaims the domestic sphere for Michael by having his baby. It is as if the infinitessimal embryo floating in Hope's uterus functions as one large maternal anchor, grounding Hope firmly within the domestic sphere once again and putting an end to Michael's deepest fears about the loss of this universe.

The episode concludes with Michael re-affirming his hitherto questionable faith in God by returning to temple after many years and saying a prayer for his dead father, whose unveiling (the Jewish practice of visiting the grave of the deceased person one year after the death) he is supposed to attend the next day. God, the father, the family, and the domestic sphere are all resurrected in Michael's life by the realization that his wife is not dying but pregnant and that he himself has planted the seed of a new life and the reproduction of a stable family order.

In sum, although the ostensible theme of the show concerns the reawakening of Michael's religious faith after Hope's accident, I would argue that it is Michael's belief in the family, not God, that is ultimately revealed as the most important spiritual value on *thirtysomething*.[2] For the domestic sphere is inscribed in the show as the centerpiece of a stable and coherent world in modern times (unlike faith in God, which in the twentieth century has been irretrievably called into question), and threats to that sphere, represented most clearly by Hope's accident, bring on attendant existential crises for the character of Michael.

To the degree that traditional gender roles serve to buttress the domestic sphere for the characters on *thirtysomething*, the show reveals itself as echoing many baby boomers' own hidden fears about what the loss of women from this sphere will mean for the family. Of course, most viewers do not have to contend with the potential death of their spouse to represent symbolically their own fears about threats to the family. Yet we would do well to recall Leo Lowenthal's assertion that "mass culture is psychoanalysis in reverse"—that it is through looking at popular culture that we can analyze what contemporary struggles are going on during a specific historical period (cited in Jay 1973:173). We can also apply Theodor Adorno's assertion about psychoanalysis to *thirtysomething* and say, "in mass culture, nothing is true except the exaggerations" (cited in Jay 1973).

The Trouble with Hope: Conflicts over Work and Family on *thirtysomething*

In its weekly synopsis, *TV Guide* characterized the 1988 premiere episode of the second season of *thirtysomething* as being about Hope's decision whether to have another child. Interestingly enough, no mention is made of the fact that this episode also portrays Hope going back to work after staying home with her first child, Janey, for twenty months. Hope's conflict in this episode thus centers on her decision whether to try to revive her career or have another child, as Michael would like her to do.

What are we to make of this conflict the creators of *thirtysomething* have constructed for the character of Hope, a conflict that is of such importance that it provides the storyline for the season's opening episode? Most female viewers were not in the position of being able to choose between home and career (as Hope can). Consequently this episode offers important insights into how *thirtysomething* was framing work and domesticity issues for women.

For the men of *thirtysomething*, conflicts over work and family are related to the ability to fulfill the traditional male role of breadwinner. The male characters are fearful that they will somehow have less control if their wives work because the women will no longer be financially dependent on them. For women, on the other hand, going to work is portrayed as fraught with psychic conflicts over transgressing traditional roles of wife and mother, as well as guilt about "abandoning" their families. At the same time, there is the sense that to hold a job is to have some kind of adult status in the world and to be respected in a way that is often lacking when they are home full time.

In order to understand how *thirtysomething* frames the problem of work for women, it may be helpful to analyze in some detail the second season's opening. Throughout the episode, Hope grapples with the decision whether to have another child or continue working, and Michael is shown as pressuring her to have another child. Thus the husband is brought in, with his needs and desires, essentially to up the emotional ante for Hope: by holding back from having another baby, she must not only deal with her own conflicting emotions but with the guilt of not being able to make Michael happy. The story unfolds, then, in terms of the conflict between Michael, who wants another child, and Hope, who wants to resume her career as a researcher for a magazine.

In the opening scenes, Hope's conflict over working or having another child is not immediately apparent. In fact, Michael appears extremely supportive of Hope's re-entry into the workworld. In the opening scene, Michael, Hope, Nancy, and Gary are gathered in Hope's and Michael's kitchen. Hope is getting ready for her first day back on the job and she is once again running around, hitting the sink as it rattles and telling Michael she will call the veterinarian after Gary says the pet looks sick. While Hope is going to work, then, we still see her focusing on the domestic world, and it takes her husband to clue us into what Hope's franticness is really about: he tells her that her ideas are great and her boss will be sure to put them in the "pipeline." The "pipeline" is linguistically contrasted with the leaking sink, or literal "pipeline," which Hope is obsessing over. Michael is thus aware of the more important "pipeline" of the outside world of work, which he assures her she will do just fine in.

In this same scene, Hope expresses her gratitude to Nancy for offering to babysit Janey. Michael asks what happened to the daycare center they had arranged for, and Hope tells him that the center's kitchen has had an outbreak of salmonella poisoning and was shut down four days earlier. This discussion about daycare is revealing in two respects. In the first place, we become aware that Michael is out of the childcare loop, indicating that it has been Hope's responsibility to come up with a childcare alternative in her own absence. In the second place, we get the feeling that outside daycare, and ultimately outside alternatives to the traditional nuclear family where the mother takes care of her own child, are somehow unreliable, and a mother figure (Nancy) is necessary as a stand-in when outside alternatives are shown to be deficient. Again, the implication is that the mother has primary responsibility for the care and development of her child.[3] Since Hope cannot be a full-time mother now, another Mom is needed. For the remainder of the episode, Nancy plays the role of muse of motherhood, the domestic figure with whom Hope identifies as she struggles with the decision to have another child. By going back to work, Hope is relinquishing her motherhood status, which she usually shares with Nancy, and thus her frantic mood can also be understood as stemming from her guilt over both ceding and dumping this responsibility onto Nancy.

In the next scene we see how Michael's initial enthusiasm for Hope's return to work is overshadowed by his own desire to have another child, coupled with his fears about being able to support that child.The scene opens with Michael and Elliot at their office, an advertising agency that they own and run together. The first thing Elliot tells Michael when he walks in is that a mutual friend of theirs has just had a baby, and he gives the exact birth weight. Michael's and Elliot's office, we understand, is itself a "homey" environment, where matters of domestic life are comfortably discussed.[4]

In response, Michael tells Elliot how great that is. He then asks where Jenine, the secretary, is; she has been on vacation and is supposed to be back. Elliot informs him that Jenine went on a game show while on vacation, and won so much money that she has quit her job. Michael then remarks that they did not even get a chance to fire her.[5] At one level, this comment about the secretary re-establishes the worklike nature of the office, where Michael is clearly the boss and concerned with where his workers are. At another level, there is the hint of an unconscious equation he is making between losing control over a woman in one area of his life (his secretary) and losing control at home as well when Hope goes back to work and "quits" her maternal role. Michael then begins to reveal what has been on his mind by asking how many children the couple they had just been discussing now have. He explains that he and Hope are thinking about having a second child, justifying this prospect by saying that because he grew up in a family with two kids, having two children is his idea of a family. When Michael complains that Janey is already twenty months old, Elliot teases him about his concerns, saying "There's a law that says that you have to have a baby in the house at all times."

This remark, although said humorously, nevertheless invokes an almost legal (social) requirement that young couples should have babies. The social framework the characters find themselves in lends legitimacy to this feeling that they are violating some social law by having only one child. This invocation of law is further bolstered when Elliot brings in a biological argument: "It's instinct, propagate the species." Again, we know this is humorous, yet the idea is nevertheless conveyed about how natural is the impulse to have children. Elliot counters his own social and biological arguments in favor of a second child, however, by bringing in the reality principle: he asks Michael if he knows how much a good pre-school costs these days. Michael responds by saying he can borrow the money from Jenine.

This vaguely misogynist comment, however, also reveals what may really be at stake. Michael's fears about making enough money to have a child may call into question his very manhood; in fantasy, at least, he has to debase himself by asking a woman—in fact, an incompetent woman—for money. Put in other terms, Michael's sense of impotence over loss of control over the actions of the women in his life (who quit jobs, or have more money than he, or leave his home to go out and work) is further exacerbated by his symbolic impotence at possibly not having enough money to father another child.

Such fears are echoed in a later scene in which Michael and Elliot fulminate against a temporary secretary they have hired to replace Jenine. The temporary secretary is portrayed as humorless and is seen typing ferociously when Elliot walks in. In an anti-realist gesture, Michael and Elliot pick up two stun-guns from their desks and shoot the secretary. We see a flash of green light as the secretary gets zapped into oblivion. Elliot defends killing her by saying, "A man's got to do what a man's got to do, Mike." Michael replies that a "man's got to sell floor wax." Elliot then begins to try to come up with ideas for selling floor wax: "All right, you miserable housewives, use this floor wax." Hostility toward women seems to abound in this vignette, as it merges with anxiety over coming up with a good idea to sell floor wax to women, which will allow Michael to be a breadwinner and father a child.

A final example of how the themes of control over women, fears about earning money, and fathering children all merge occurs in another scene at Michael's and Elliot's office, which at this point in the episode has been transformed from a "child-centered" environment to the functional equivalent of a men's locker room. In this scene, Michael tells Elliot that they need to come up with an idea for floor wax because they need to earn money. Elliot replies that he cannot be expected to come up with any ideas because he is separated from his wife, Nancy. Again, the theme of loss of control over women is connected with inability to be a breadwinner. When Michael asks how she is, Elliot replies, "Shrewlike, vindictive, I miss her." Michael then observes, "Women, you can't live with them, you can't kill them." New Age men, indeed.

Sensing that there must be some problem at home, Elliot asks Michael what Hope "did now." Michael admits that the night before, while they were involved in foreplay, Hope went to get her diaphragm, which upset Michael. Michael asks if it is a crime to be upset, "because one kid doesn't feel like a family to me" and points out that Elliot has two kids. Elliot tells him:

> Yeah, but that was part of our pre-nuptual agreement. She agreed to have two kids and serve my every whim and I agreed to systematically destroy her self-esteem and all of her confidence.

In one sense, this quote typifies *thirtysomething*'s loudly proclaimed *solidarity* with feminist verities (such as, what the patriarchal family does to women). But such insights are tossed off with knowing, ironic humor *like everything else,* and hence have little impact in themselves; the real drift lies elsewhere. For example, although Michael knows this is said humorously, he replies almost wistfully to Elliott, "Maybe you were smart."

For Hope, on the other hand, the decision to have another child is not bound up with her potential ability to earn enough money to support the child so much as a desire to reclaim her identity as a working woman. In the scene immediately following Michael's and Elliot's first discussion, we see Hope with her boss Valerie, at the offices of the magazine where she works as a researcher. She asks her boss whether she likes the ideas she brought in for magazine articles. Valerie says she likes some of them but that the magazine has already done many of the stories, and wonders whether Hope has even read the magazine in her maternity absence. Hope tells her that all she's been able to keep up with is *Curious George,* a children's book. It is clear where Hope has been, namely, doing full-time childcare, and while the remark is a joke, the implication is clear that being a full-time mother has caused her to fall behind in her field.

After this admission, Valerie asks Hope for the latest "photo opportunities." At first, as Hope fumbles through her folder where her work is, we assume that the boss means pictures for the magazine articles, but then the camera reveals that they are looking at pictures of Janey. The effect of this move is to humanize the boss as a maternal figure herself, who furthermore has a sense of children as the "real" priorities in life, as well as to offer Hope a momentary feeling of being re-grounded as a mother herself.[6] Now that the situation is re-humanized in relation to women's non-work roles, Hope's boss goes on to comment on how Janey does not even look like a baby any more and how fast they grow up. This comment subtly echoes the earlier conversation between Michael and Elliot, where not even children, but specifically babies, were described as the cultural goal. As if to reinforce this notion that having a baby is a cultural ideal, Valerie asks Hope if she is going to have another kid.[7] Hope expresses her ambivalence about motherhood by saying that she is still trying to get Payroll to spell her name right on her first paycheck, indicating her feeling that she is still trying to get her feet back in the workplace after her first child. The situation thus subtly sets up Hope so that her boss is viewing her in terms of being a mother precisely at the moment she is trying to reassert herself as a working woman.

The conflict between work and having another child is most clearly expressed in a scene that occurs toward the end of the episode. The scene opens with Michael returning from work. He greets Hope, who throughout the episode has been having difficulty writing the article she was assigned to do. He asks her how her writing is going, and she explains to him that because of a variety of household events, she could not get any work done. After listing the litany of household chores she has done, Hope comments sarcastically, "So, I got a lot of work done." Michael responds in an unsupportive way, "So write," and then asks her morosely whether he should pick up dinner on his way back from meeting his friend Gary. Realizing he has sounded somewhat less than supportive, he begins "I know this is a bad time." Hope tells him:

> It's not a bad time, it's a busy time, it's a difficult time. Look, do you know how good it feels to be back at work? To feel like I'm contributing? To feel like people aren't shaking their heads as if I'm wasting my life?

Rather than respond to Hope's point about how much it means to her to be back working, Michael undercuts her efforts by saying, "But you're not even writing it." Realizing that Michael is expressing some deeper grievance, Hope asks him, "What does that mean?" He replies, "It seems like you're having this incredibly difficult time writing it and yet you claim to be happy." Hope then gives voice to what she thinks Michael is really saying, and responds, "And you thought I'd be happier if I got pregnant again?" When Michael denies this, Hope continues, "What you're really saying is that you'd be happier if I got pregnant again." Once Hope has given voice to what is really at stake in this discussion about her difficulty getting back to work again, Michael tries to defend himself by saying, "I don't believe you, yes Hope and barefoot too. I mean what do you think I am?"

Hope tries to backpedal from the conflict by explaining that going back to work makes her feel like she is finally taking charge of her destiny again after losing her confidence from being home with the baby. Finally acknowledging the reality of what Hope has been trying to tell him, he plaintively asks, "So, this isn't a good time to have another baby?" Hope answers yes, then asks him, "You really want to have another one?" Michael answers, at this point disingenuously, "No."

It is not without irony that the interchange takes place while Hope is holding Janey's doll: what is at stake is ultimately not so much even being a mother as trying to regain some kind of adult status in the world. That Hope realizes that having a part-time job probably does not seem like much to other people does not obviate the importance it holds for her as a way to re-enter the adult world after having children.

While for Michael the greatest problem associated with having another baby is whether he can support the family financially, for Hope the problem is trying to reclaim her earlier identity as an adult whose actions mean something in the world.

The episode is resolved by Hope's deciding to have another child. How does Hope move from her original resistance and commitment to a career to deciding to try to get pregnant again? Two major themes lead to the decision. For one thing, throughout the episode Hope has been procrastinating doing her writing by reading a journal and looking at snapshots of a couple from World War II that she has discovered in an old chest in her basement. As Hope looks at a photograph of the couple, the snapshot suddenly comes alive, and Hope realizes that her house at one time belonged to them. This realization triggers a series of flashbacks throughout the rest of the episode, as Hope compares her own life to that of the woman from the photograph. As we have seen, nostalgia for earlier times is invoked as a recurring theme throughout the show, and in this instance, Hope's flashbacks of this woman interweave with her ultimate decision to have another child.[8]

Hope follows the course of the woman's courtship and subsequent marriage to a soldier. The woman gets pregnant by the soldier during his leave and then miscarries the child. Hope is completely broken up over the woman's loss, and appears to identify not only with the loss but with the feeling that her life too is out of control. Hope's feeling of being out of control is grounded in the episode's second theme: Hope's discovery that her home has a high reading of radon, an invisible, poisonous gas.

Having made the identification between the woman and herself in terms of their feeling alone and out of control, Hope reflects that the woman became a nurse because it was wartime, but that "we can do whatever we want." She continues:

> I try to have a career, but in the end it just doesn't make any difference, because we can't control things any more than they could.

Hope then tells Michael, "Oh, Michael, I'm so tired," as she puts her head on his shoulder. In this scene, it is clear that Hope has been making the connection between having control over her life and going back to work. When she discovers that she has no ultimate control over her life, as evidenced by radon seeping into her home, she seems ready to throw in the towel and relinquishes control to Michael by putting her head literally on his shoulders.

The episode concludes with Hope reading that the woman gets pregnant again and then goes out to the garden to plant roses for both her children. The woman, in other words, resolves her own feelings of being alone and out of control by getting pregnant again. Pregnancy on *thirtysomething* is thus meant to symbolize feeling hope in a hostile world as well as reclaiming control and order. When the woman tells Hope to "take care of the garden, it's yours now," the implication is clear that Hope can regain control of her life, can regain Hope, by herself having another child. In general, then, the implication is that for women to regain a sense of control in their lives, simply going back to work is not enough. Rather, they can ultimately center themselves by reclaiming their original role as childbearers.

The last scene ends somewhat ambivalently along these lines, as Hope goes out to the garden. It is late at night and Michael follows her there, bringing her a blanket to keep her warm. He tells her that they can begin to try to revive the rose bushes over the weekend and that they have to make time to do so. Hope tells him, "This is a good house, we might have a little invisible poison gas." Michael replies, "So we'll start this weekend to make the time," apparently referring to the garden. Hope answers, "We'll start right now"; she takes off her nightgown and they embrace. The implication is that Hope is ready to try to conceive another child. The last shot shows a picture of the house, and Hope's voiceover tells us that she is beginning her own journal for the next tenant to read. She begins, "Her name is . . . my name is Hope."

By portraying the character of Hope as being in conflict over work versus family, *thirtysomething* taps into an existential dilemma that the great majority of women could be said to be going through, namely, how to piece together a sense of self amid a clash between traditional gender roles as wives and mothers and identities as working women. In Hope's case, the show tries to resolve the conflict by making the psychic rewards of having a child, with the attendant control gained over her life, greater than working. Unfortunately, the problem will not go away so easily. For as long as women are required by either economic necessity or desire for personal fulfillment, or both, to be out in the workforce, they will have to come to terms with what this means for their traditional roles as wives and mothers.

Theme of Reconciliation with Motherhood

Another theme that recurs throughout *thirtysomething* involves women's coming to terms with their roles as mothers. While it might seem that the status of motherhood would be most clearly addressed in the two married women who are mothers, in many ways it is more instructive to analyze how this issue is treated in the construction of the two female characters who are both unmarried and childless, Melissa and Ellyn. To see why Melissa and Ellyn have problematic lives is to view *thirtysomething*'s implicit assumptions about what mothers should be like.

This analysis of the single female characters reveals what may be described as *thirtysomething*'s hidden teleological framework, which measures all women against a model of female maturity defined, by and large, by their acceptance of the mothering role. This "hidden" framework, in turn, reflects prevailing assumptions in the larger culture that define women in terms of their capacity to "mother" others. In order to see how these issues are portrayed, it will be helpful to discuss briefly the character of Melissa as a potential "mother," and then to analyze in some detail an episode that concerns Ellyn's coming to terms with her own mothering capacities.

Melissa Steadman

Although the character Melissa seems destined to be forever without a husband or family, she is nevertheless often shown as very loving and giving. Melissa is the warm, nurturing, "nice Jewish girl" on the show who would probably make the best Mom of all, if only she could get a man to have a child with. Melissa's mothering capacities are portrayed in a variety of ways. In one episode, for example, like the spinster aunt she is sometimes meant to portray symbolically, Melissa teaches Ethan, Nancy's pre-pubescent son, how to dance. This tutelage allows Ethan to exercise his Oedipal fantasies safely with an older woman while at the same time allowing Melissa to play-act the role of a mother/lover initiating her son into heterosexual activities like slow dancing. As if to reinforce the sexual elements behind this mother/son initiation, Ethan is learning this dance because he is to play Prince Charming in the school play, and thus the underlying message is that he is Melissa's Prince Charming.[9]

What is most interesting in terms of the issue of mothering is that one gets the feeling, after seeing Melissa placed in these awkward roles as the lover/mother to younger men, is that somehow a warm, caring, nurturing Jewish woman is by definition a mothering woman, and thus all her relationships will be characterized by this mothering role.[10] For example, in one episode where Hope and Michael make a will and have to name a guardian for their child (air date Feb. 20, 1990), Melissa is finally chosen among all their friends, including their married ones, thereby indicating that, were it not for her unfortunate condition of being without a man, Melissa could indeed be an excellent parent.

Besides looking as if she might have been a good mother to the other adults on the show, Melissa in fact looks like she would be the kind of Mom whom other children wish they could have had, perhaps because she herself is shown to be so childlike. Her childlike qualities are emphasized by her comical clothing, by her changing hair color, by her perpetual inability to have an adult, heterosexual relationship, and finally by her literal infantilization by her parents. In one episode she is shown, in another anti-realist gesture, literally shrinking into a small child in her father's office, where she is ostensibly meeting with him and his lawyer to buy the loft where she lives. Of course these childlike qualities that are given to Melissa, Gary, and Elliot in various episodes, and that could be said to be constitutive features of their personalities, are also meant to denote their immaturity and inability to face up to the adult responsibilities of life, which in Melissa's case would be marriage and motherhood.

Thus Melissa's warmth and caregiving abilities are ultimately thwarted by her lack of maturity, which conspires to deny her her real potential for happiness. In an episode on singles dating Melissa's definition of happiness is jokingly identified as "being married and having fights with your husband on long car trips." So, on a scale of one to ten, Melissa's mothering potential scores a five, always a possibility but never reaching full scope, which would mean being in a nuclear family with a real husband and children.

Ellyn Warren

If Melissa exists somewhere in the middle of the spectrum in terms of her mothering capacities, Ellyn stands clearly at the incapacitated end of the scale. Her incapacity is connected to her representation as a career woman, and the implicit message is that to be a career woman in effect somehow precludes being a mother. This dichotomy between career woman and mother is brought home in the episode in which Hope and Michael are planning their will. In considering Ellyn, who is Hope's oldest friend, Hope and Michael try to imagine what Ellyn would be like as Janey's mother. In yet another anti-realist sequence—these sequences often clue us into the characters' real fears and obsessions, and thus seem to function as the characters' neurotic daydreams—we see Ellyn and Janey in corporate "power suits," both acting the part of the stereotyped high-powered career women: Janey, in fact, is a pint-sized version of Ellyn's career woman, dressed in an identical outfit and behaving exactly like Ellyn. The fear, for Hope and Michael, is that Janey will turn into Ellyn, or more precisely become Ellyn's type of career woman, self-absorbed, neurotic, driven. The implication is that this is the worst case scenario for their daughter's future.

Besides her rampant careerism, Ellyn is also not perceived as motherly because she routinely acts out the role of vixen/slut, and this hypersexuality is contrasted with the asexual maternal qualities of Hope and Nancy. While prostitutes are sometimes allowed to be mothers in our cultural folklore (those with hearts of gold at least), mothers are usually not allowed to be sexual, and Ellyn as vixen has neither a child to be maternal toward nor the likelihood of becoming a mother. Ellyn's vixenhood is expressed in a variety of ways: she is often shown wearing skimpy clothes, as in the opening credits, where she sits in her psychiatrist's office wearing a tight purple tank top, her legs suggestively crossed; when she goes shopping with Hope and Melissa, we see her picking out the sexiest underwear to Hope's and Melissa's horrified yet titillated delight; her voice is deep and husky and she has a tattoo on her backside; and finally, she has an affair with a married man, Jeffrey, whose wife, on finding out about the affair, says frantically to Hope and Michael, "I mean she was kind of slutty at your party but I had no idea what kind of a person she was" (episode where Jeffrey leaves his wife and moves into Ellyn's).

If Melissa is the good-natured, yet slightly de-sexualized female character who prefers cotton "lollipop" underwear, Ellyn is the career woman whose silk lingerie lurks just beneath the surface of her tailored, padded-shouldered suits and demeanor. Of course, the linking of Ellyn with both careerism and rampant sexuality, at first seemingly opposite traits, reflects the reality that in our culture work and sex can never be separated. Even Hope has to struggle with her sexual feelings for a coworker in one episode, and Ellyn later has an affair with her boss.

In terms of the problem of motherhood, Ellyn's hyper-sexuality and careerism at first eliminate her from the spectrum of motherhood itself. During one episode of the final season, however, Ellyn comes close to being reconciled with her own mothering potential. This reconciliation is portrayed as a mark of maturity for an otherwise hopelessly neurotic and immature character. Ellyn's domestication occurs in an episode in which her married lover, Jeffrey, finally agrees to leave his wife and moves in with Ellyn with his daughter Christie and his dog. Ellyn is thereby transformed into a de facto stepmother to Jeffrey's family.

In the opening scene we see Ellyn coming into her apartment, rushing around as if quickly getting ready for a guest. It is in the middle of the day and she is wearing her tailored suit, indicating that she has come home from work during her lunch hour. She quickly picks up a pile of laundry on the floor of her otherwise immaculate apartment as she simultaneously cajoles and yells at her cat. The laundry in an otherwise spotless apartment seems to signify that in Ellyn's world the only lived-in things are her clothes, work clothes, which she is so busy working in that she does not even have them laundered.

As Ellyn rushes around, the doorbell rings and we see what she has been hurrying for: Jeffrey is there to rendezvous with her for an hour of lovemaking. The mutually exciting nature of this tryst is underscored by the tearing off of their clothes as they stumble toward the bed. Clearly, there is nothing domestic about this arrangement. Immediately *après* sex, Jeffrey hurriedly dresses as Ellyn lies in the bed, and they both begin concocting hypothetical excuses to tell co-workers for why they are so late from lunch. Jeffrey then goes over to Ellyn and shows him a picture of himself, his dog, and his daughter Christie. Ellyn dissolves in tears, saying "I didn't even know you had a dog!" thereby indicating that she has no sense of his domestic life, and then defensively and abruptly tells him that she has to leave to write a report at work. Her need to go to work and write a report is mentioned again later in the show, also as a defensive reaction, when she sees Hope and has difficulty dealing with the emotional nature of the encounter. Ellyn's need to go work somehow itself has the character of defense, suggesting that work for some women is a defense against some psychic disturbance they are experiencing.[11]

After this opening scene, where Ellyn expresses her unhappiness at their illicit relationship, the rest of the episode focuses on Jeffrey's subsequent decision to leave his wife for Ellyn and his and Ellyn's attempts to make the transition from lovers to a domesticated couple. In this transition, the issue of motherhood revolves around the problem of Jeffrey's daughter. Initially, Ellyn does not seem able to deal with the reality of the daughter as part of the life she will be inheriting in getting together with Jeffrey. This reluctance is further revealed in her conversations with her psychiatrist, whom she is shown speaking with in alternate scenes throughout the episode.

In her first conversation with her therapist, she relates that Jeffrey is indeed leaving his wife for her. Explaining the difficulties attending this, she expresses her insecurity that men do not stay with the woman whom they leave their wives for. She feels like the attempt is doomed: "It's really complicated . . . he's got this dog." The therapist then interjects, "Hasn't he got a daughter?" indicating that Ellyn was blocking the significant fact of Jeffrey's life, namely his daughter. She then replies, "Yeah. It's really complicated. Her real mother is in Saudi Arabia and her stepmother has call waiting where her heart should be."

In this exchange, both previous mothers are revealed to be somehow inadequate, with one being in a foreign country and the other being even more of a hyper-career woman than Ellyn herself. The fact that the other two women are incompetent mothers raises the question of Ellyn's competence in mothering the girl. Motherhood is understood in this scene to be a problem for Ellyn precisely because the daughter appears motherless without her.

Ellyn's reluctance to accept the mother role is expressed in a variety of ways. For example, when Jeffrey checks into a hotel room when he first leaves his wife, Ellyn and the daughter are there with him. Ellyn suggests that he call a concierge to babysit for Christie so that she and Jeffrey can have some time alone together, and he replies in amazement, "I couldn't do that to her now," meaning so soon after he has left his wife and their home. At another point, when she talks to her therapist, she says, somewhat defensively, "Everything's great, everything's terrific. We haven't made love in six and a half days, because we haven't had any actual time alone together." Her relation with his daughter is awkward at best, non-existent at worst.

Continuing with this line of questioning, the therapist asks, "You met the daughter?" She replies, "Yes." He then asks, "How did you find her?" "Right next to him!" Her quips are a form of resistance to talking about the daughter and she and the therapist discuss her need to make quips. She says she thinks she acted badly, though "not morally wrong, like stealing. I wasn't being myself, but like Cherry Ames, student nurse." Ellyn continues this stream-of-consciousness monologue by commenting on how when she was younger she once stole a true confession magazine, one of the ones where the girls either get raped or go out with married men. She tells the therapist this was the only thing she ever stole, "except Jeffrey."

For Ellyn, guilt and sexuality are linked through her stealing of a "true confession magazine" at puberty that contained stories about stealing married men. The act is symbolically repeated in her adult life, in her affair with a married man. Her sexuality, it seems, is stuck at an earlier immature stage, puberty or the Oedipal stage itself, as represented by her desire to "steal" a married man, symbolically understood as her father. The implication of her confession to her therapist is subtle yet complex: in stealing Jeffrey she is reliving her Oedipal guilt at her desire to "steal" her father (a married man) from her mother. This guilt precludes her from herself becoming a mother, because she is stuck at this earlier, infantile stage of reacting to her primary Oedipal guilt.[12]

To be a mother to Jeffrey's daughter would be tantamount for Ellyn, to replacing her own mother in the Oedipal triangle. Put in other terms, the discussion with her therapist reveals that, because Ellyn still perceives herself as a little girl who wants her father and feels guilty about her mother, she is in no position to assume the role of mother herself. What lends credence to this interpretation is a later scene in the same episode where Ellyn confesses to Hope, the maternal figure in her life, that Jeffrey left his wife for her. Fearing Hope's judgmental reaction, she is enormously relieved when Hope does not act surprised and in fact seems to accept the situation. She tells Hope, "You don't know how much this means to me." This indicates that she has somehow been able, through Hope, to expiate her guilt at stealing a man (father) and can thus begin to make the progression toward mature female sexuality and presumably motherhood.

What clearly helps Ellyn along in this transition from child to mother is her own recognition that she sees a lot of herself in Christie, Jeffrey's child, not so much in terms of their Oedipal desires as in their feeling of being unwanted or unloved. This identification occurs at two points. At one point she reveals to her therapist, "Let's face it, it would be easier if she [Christie] didn't exist." This comment mirrors Ellyn's own feelings that her parents would have been better off if she had not existed, as when she explains to Christie that her own parents separated because they were trying to "find themselves or lose themselves, or lose me in a crowd." In a later scene, the connections between her own feelings of being unloved by her mother and Christie's situation are again linked, as she describes to her therapist the fight that occurred earlier in Jeffrey's office between Jeffrey and his second wife, the stepmother, commenting that they acted as if "she [Christie] didn't even exist, even though she was standing right there." Ellyn then explains to the therapist what happened when she was younger, when she looked through her mother's drawers to try to find the magazine she had stolen. She admits that she continued to search her mother's drawers even after she realized her mother had not put the magazine there because she was "looking for some tangible proof that would make you believe her . . . believe her when she tells you that she loves you, because something's missing and you don't know what it is." Ellyn's inability to experience her mother's love, her feeling that something was missing between her mother and her, is poignantly linked to Christie's own non-personhood in the eyes of her parents. In effect, this identification between Christie and herself, invoked through Ellyn's stream of consciousness monologue to her therapist, tells us the real nature of Ellyn's defensiveness against inheriting Jeffrey's domestic life: through Christie, she must relive her own childhood traumas of being unloved and unwanted by her own mother as she tries to fit into a life in which there does not seem to be a place for her.

Immediately after this heartwrenching admission, Ellyn continues, "His daughter left something today. I have something she needs." She then begins to cry. "Why does that make you cry?" her therapist asks. "Because it's just so stupid. She loses everything. She loses everything." Ostensibly, Ellyn is referring to Christie's notebook, a written stream of consciousness (paralleling Ellyn's stream of consciousness to her therapist) that her teacher had asked the students to keep in a journal. At another level, Ellyn is crying because she recognizes that, like Ellyn herself, Christie essentially needs to be loved and that, furthermore, it is she who can give Christie (and implicitly herself) the love her mother never gave her. "I have something she needs." Ellyn's maturity (in the form of her therapeutic recognition) is linked to her transition from identifying with the scared, unloved Christie to wanting to give love to Christie, from wanting to be mothered herself to wanting to give Christie the mothering she herself never felt.

This desire to give Christie the love she never felt from her own mother is expressed in the closing scenes of the episode where she tells Christie, "I don't even know if I like you, but apparently I love you," to which Christie then replies, "The thing is I already have a mother and she's really great." Unfazed by this admission, Ellyn replies, "I don't want to be your mother I don't know how to be anybody's mother." Christie then asks, "You really love me?" Ellen responds, "Yeah."

Ultimately, Ellyn's ability to love Christie, and implicitly to give love to that part of herself that identifies with Christie, symbolizes Ellyn's reconciliation with her maternal urges. We know that Ellyn will never be the mother figure that Hope and Nancy represent, and in fact Ellyn herself is the first to admit that she does not know how to be anybody's mother. Still, her admission signals that she has reached a new level of insight into her emotions and is psychically prepared to be able to give love to a child, to mother if not exactly to be a mother. This newfound emotional maturity is echoed in the closing scenes of this episode, where we see Ellyn reach a new acceptance of the domestication of her life. After this scene with Christie, they all return to Ellyn's apartment where Jeffrey's dog has been left alone. Ellyn's apartment has been the single girl's paradise, where every expensive item has its place and where most of the domestic items, such as pots and pans, go permanently unused. They find her apartment in complete disarray. Rather than being upset, Ellyn cheerfully defends the dog, as if to say, I now accept the chaos that having a family will inevitably bring to my life. I am now a mature woman who can accommodate myself to others: in short, my home is now fit for a family.

SUMMARY

Much recent feminist literature has focused on re-exploring women's roles as mothers. This literature tends to re-valorize the activity of mothering, which feminists had presumably downplayed in their earlier efforts to change women's gender roles in society. Rather than assign to one specific sex the role of mothering, these feminists argue that mothering should be considered a highly valued and gender neutral activity.

While the ideal that both sexes should be able to assume a variety of roles in the family, including sharing the role of mothering, so that it might appropriately be re-defined as parenting, is an important goal, that day is not yet with us. Instead, our culture is still characterized by the often not so hidden assumption that mothering, whether psychically or practically, is a woman's job. Not only is this role still primarily occupied by women, but contemporary cultural discourses, in general, tend to reinforce this practice by, in a sense, measuring all women against the cultural ideal of motherhood.

Conclusion

One of the primary claims of Edward Zwick and Marshall Herskovitz, as we saw, is that their program mirrors the real-life experiences of their audiences. Concurring with this assessment that the show tends to mirror the real lives of people that they know, the writers, directors, and even actors on *thirtysomething* always emphasized the ways in which the show is "incontrovertibly really *real*" (Herman 1988:46). As Sasha Torres has pointed out, there are virtually no reviews of the program that do not touch on its supposed realism or ability to track the real lives of its audience (Torres 1989).

In general, this emphasis on "real life" in recent television programs geared toward the boomer generation, while part of a broader network marketing strategy at the time, also stemmed from a much longer tradition in the history of television, one that has always focused on the characters' emotional state and the everyday struggles that they face in their day-to-day lives. Commenting on this tradition in television, Ella Taylor (1988) has drawn parallels to the novel form, and finds that television functions as a kind of modern bard chronicling our everyday concerns (Taylor 1988:H39).

Although the creators of *thirtysomething* claim that they were trying to mirror the social reality of their viewers, much recent writing on television has criticized this belief in the ability of television somehow to faithfully reproduce social reality. Taylor notes, for example,

> In no period . . . does television imagery of family or workplace mirror real conditions of living, though it may, by virtue of its celebration of the ordinary and its mimetic form, appear to do so. (Taylor 1989:153)

If television cannot be said simply to mirror social reality, what are we to make of *thirtysomething*'s claim that it realistically portrays, through distinct storylines, the "real lives" of its viewers? One way we can begin to answer this question is to point out, as John Fiske does, that television, as a mainstream cultural medium, is able to reproduce the dominant *sense* of reality through the conventional devices of the dramatic form of realism itself (Fiske 1989). By dealing with a content that is about ordinary actions in the world, and by positioning its viewers to "read" these actions from the viewpoint of an ideal or real narrator, realist dramas help to re-create the viewers' world within a recognizable system (Belsey 1980).

Ultimately, while *thirtysomething* was arguably successful in charting its viewers' *sense* of their social reality, the ways in which the program resolved women's conflicts in a conservative direction clouded viewers' ability to imagine that their social reality could change. For *thirtysomething* foreclosed alternative ways of resolving crises over gender, and generally went in a conservative direction in the solutions it posed. In the next chapter we will explore how women responded to these solutions, in terms of both their reactions to the program and their reflections on their own life choices.

Notes

1. As if to reinforce Gary's point, the characters each then go on to trace their own earlier assumptions about the world through reminiscences of these shows. For example, Ellyn, the female character who is neurotic, single, and often shown visiting her psychiatrist, remarks on how she always thought it was curious that the mothers on some of these shows were dead or absent and that the children were subsequently raised by bachelor fathers and uncles. Recalling these domestic situa-

tions, she reflected that when she fought with her own mother she often wished the same fate would happen to her.

Although recalled humorously, this remembrance nevertheless indicates to the audience why Ellyn's own domestic arrangement lacks a traditional nuclear unit. In addition, the idea is subtly reinforced that Ellyn herself is unmotherly: wishing to kill her mother when she was younger is not exactly the sentiment evoked by someone who might herself want to be a mother someday. We never hear Hope or Nancy, for example, the two mother figures on the show, making this kind of admission.

Michael continues the reminiscences by commenting on how he was always confused by how Chip, from *My Three Sons*, could start his own business and be wildly successful one week and then the next week flunk out of school. This remembrance in effect mirrors his own current anxieties about the fate of his business, which is shown in earlier episodes as failing. Furthermore, in terms of gender roles, it establishes that even in his youth Michael viewed himself in the role of breadwinner and already evidenced anxiety about potential failure. For all Ellyn's career woman status on the show, for example, she never identifies with Chip's business ventures (because work for women is not conceptualized on the show primarily in terms of financial gain), yet it is entirely conceivable that Michael would have been making these connections between being a breadwinner and fearing potential failure, even at an early age.

Finally Hope, the maternal figure on the show, remarks, "I love tv—everybody's always nice and everybody's always happy." At one level, we know that Hope knows that reality is not like this and is thus mocking the forms of television, yet at another level we hear the wish fulfillment in her voice for life to in fact be like this. Reinforcing this view, she then smiles shyly at Michael, as if to say, "We have indeed created this happy world for ourselves, despite the others' unhappiness."

2. In the show, Hope's accident makes Michael realize how much he loves her and how little control he has over his world. The return to God, in the form of going to the temple and saying a prayer (*yahrzheit*) for his father's death, represents a return to tradition in its deepest sense: to combat the vicissitudes of modern life and the encroachments against what is most important to him (Hope and his family), he returns to what he once rejected (God and Judaism) as a source of consolation and protection from these threats.

3. The recent hysteria over child sexual abuse in daycare centers is due, at least in part, to this cultural imperative that views the mother as the foundation of the child's biological, social, and moral development

and the attendant guilt that many women feel when leaving their children in the hands of others. The hysteria evidenced over fears of sexual misconduct plays into our culture's anxiety over leaving children in the "hands of strangers." More generally, daycare is still viewed as a patchwork solution at best: the assumption is that children get sick from other children in daycare, or that outbreaks of germs (here, salmonella) may strike at any moment, or that it is simply not as reliable as a parent taking care of one's own. In this way, *thirtysomething* accurately captured some of the fears, real and imagined, about putting children into this outside structure in the wake of women entering the workforce.

4. In the next season, when the business goes under and Michael and Elliot are forced to work for another agency, the male office environment gets re-defined in more traditional, competitive terms. But for now it is clear that the world of the family can be discussed in this friendly environment, and the birth of children is an important fact, which precedes any immediate concerns of work. Fatherhood, however it may be understood, is clearly valued here in this New Age office.

5. This remark plays into the old stereotype of the incompetent secretary with a twist. For Michael, recognizing her incompetence, would have fired her if she had not up and quit herself, thereby subverting his power as a boss. Still, we are left with the same picture of the male boss castigating the incompetent woman in the pink-collar job, even though she now has the economic power to be uppity and quit.

6. More interestingly, the work environments of both Hope and Michael are portrayed as being "child-friendly," thereby initially setting up the idea that work and family can exist harmoniously for both sexes, especially when there is some mother figure at home with the baby.

7. This is an innocent question in itself, unless we look at it in the context of its being Hope's first day back on the job.

8. Nostalgia on *thirtysomething* often functions to bring a resolution that in fact is regressive in nature: a traditional solution to a modern dilemma.

9. The theme of Melissa looking for a lover/son is further evidenced by her sexual relationship with Lee, a working-class painter approximately ten years her junior. While raising the idea that a man being with a woman ten years younger should hardly raise an eyebrow (in fact, would be a source of grudging admiration), the pairing of Melissa with a younger man does symbolically add weight to her supposed need to mother others. The quasi-tragic end to their relationship, furthermore, supposedly a result of the stresses brought about by their age difference, tends to reinforce the Oedipal taboos associated with women who have

sex with much younger men. Reinforcing this notion that the relationship violates Oedipal taboos, as we see, Melissa's mothering of Lee itself becomes a source of tension in their relationship, as when she tries to get him a job at Michael's company, mirroring her parents' own efforts to buy her the loft she lives in and give her some financial security.

10. In the *New York Times* Arts and Leisure section for July 15, 1990, in an article concerning the representation of Jewish men on prime time television (O'Connor 1990), John O'Connor stated that Melissa Steadman was the only female prime time tv character who was explicitly Jewish, and that it was only recently that Jewish men were being openly portrayed on prime time. Presumably, the fact that Melissa's Jewishness is made explicit lends weight to my making associations between her Jewishness and the Jewish Mother imago. The writers/creators of the show themselves are married to non-Jewish women, and the characters of Hope and Nancy are supposedly mirrored after their own wives, yet it is not outside the realm of possibility that the writers still have their own unconscious associations of their (Jewish) mothers with Jewish women in general.

11. One wonders whether the writers of the show would characterize their own need to write in such defensive terms, or whether they are simply trying to underscore the idea that career women's attachment to work *itself* has the character of a defense.

12. This guilt and her subsequent inability to be a mother herself is further evidenced in a later discussion with her therapist, when she relates how her mother found out about her theft by finding the magazine in Ellyn's drawer. Rather than confront her directly, the mother took the magazine and said nothing, but Ellyn nevertheless knew that "she knew that I knew that she knew that I was a sex fiend." Because of her mother's silence, however, Ellyn was denied the opportunity to work through her guilt about her curiosity about sex and lingering Oedipal desires. The implication is that Ellyn has never gotten over this guilt of her mother's knowledge of her desires, and that in her desire for Jeffrey she is reliving this guilt that her mother somehow knows and disapproves of her desire for a married man/father.

Chapter 4

Damned If You Do, Damned If You Don't: Women's Responses to Gender Conflicts on *thirtysomething*

In the previous discussions, we have looked at the historical, social, and cultural frameworks within which *thirtysomething* was generated. In addition, we have explored the gender conflicts raised on the show, at the level of character and storylines. Although these explorations are useful for our thinking about how *thirtysomething* was framed as a cultural document about women's gender roles, we must still investigate how these ideas were received by female viewers of the show. For, as the theoretical perspectives outlined in Chapter 1 indicate, it is not enough simply to explore the "texts" of television; we must also examine how audiences generate meanings through the act of viewing.

Recent scholarship in the area of feminist ethnography suggests that women use popular culture in complex ways, to open up a space to think about their own lives as they are and to construct alternative fantasies of how they might want their lives to be. These studies can help us to think through women's responses to *thirtysomething*. For female viewers of *thirtysomething* also used popular culture to help them construct a workable female identity, often by identifying with a female character's response to a gender crisis in her fictional life. In this chapter, I explore more generally how various groups of women responded to specific female characters. Then, in Chapter 5, I present profiles of six female viewers and their responses. The specific women profiled were chosen from the larger sample both because their views were echoed by many of the women in the study and because they offered a particularly eloquent expression of conflicts surrounding their own lives.

Before we attempt to summarize the reactions of female viewers generally to individual female characters, it will be helpful to raise again briefly the issue of class. I pointed out in Chapter 1 that, while I aimed my sample group at the target group *thirtysomething* was marketed toward—white, urban, middle-class viewers—it quickly became apparent that the social class "middle" is very hard to pin down. In an attempt to overcome that problem, I used as many of these variables as possible in delineating the class background of the women in my sample. In some ways, however, it is very difficult to set out with social categories and then assign individuals, a priori, to one or another group based on these categories. For, as the work of ethnography demonstrates, the way individuals actually live cannot often be traced back to any specific variable in their socio-economic background. Put in other terms, social science "assignments" of class are problematic because you cannot assume that this assignment will be stable. In this sense, it may be helpful to think of class as a *lived* category, one that is constructed through the history and lived experience of individual women. In fact, we live our class in relation to every other aspect of the social world, including pop culture. Thinking of Bourdieu's "taste cultures," for example, we see how individuals try actively to construct their experiences of class through their choices of objects from material and popular culture.

The more general point for our discussion is the idea that we need to be flexible in our understanding of class, and to interrogate it as an *open*, rather than fixed, category. As we will see in the next chapter, the individual women profiled, while coming from similar economic backgrounds, played out their lives in very different ways. More provocatively, they drew on *thirtysomething* itself as a way to articulate and define not only their gender but their class identities in very different ways. In this chapter, I will make some general statements about women from lower- and upper-middle-class backgrounds, recognizing that these assignations can never fully describe the complex ways these women constructed their class through their lived experiences. In the chapter that follows, which profiles individual women, I hope we will be able to chart that process somewhat more closely.

In general, women from lower-middle-class backgrounds tended to identify not so much with the individual female characters as with the *life situations* these characters experienced. In fact, they were often hostile to the characters themselves, seeing them as not appreciating the things they had, or as complaining endlessly when they actually had it pretty good. They were often critical of the characters' need to verbalize issues associated with their lives, or "say out loud" what they were feeling, yet they sympathized with the situations that the characters were discussing.

In addition, many lower-middle-class women distinctly perceived themselves as coming from a different class background from that of the female characters and as having different life choices available to themselves from those of the fictional characters. Thus, while they found common ground in identifying with the gender crises the female characters had, they were much more distanced from these characters in terms of assessing both how the characters needed obsessively to describe their crises and how these fictional women could resolve their difficulties.

Upper-middle-class women, on the other hand, not only identified with the situations of the female characters but also enjoyed the ways in which the characters spoke at length about these conflicts. In addition, they also felt more in common with the choices and options available to the fictional women. Thus while the lower-middle-class women generally felt that the characters "complained too much," the upper-middle-class women tended to derive enjoyment from this self-absorbed self-disclosure of the characters' inner lives.

Women's Reactions to Hope: Conflicts over Work and Family

In general, the majority of women from both the lower- and upper-middle-class groupings felt that the portrayal of Hope's conflicts over work and family were "realistic," and many of the women could empathize with her sense of frustration, whether or not they had gone through similar experiences in their own lives.[1] In describing the portrayal of Hope's conflicts as realistic, women cited the following areas as especially "true to life": (a) resentment at being the one in the marriage who has to choose between family and career; (b) anger at being the one who has to make the compromises to preserve the family peace; (c) unhappiness at putting the needs of others before her own needs; (d) loss of confidence and self-esteem in leaving the workforce and becoming a full-time mother; and (e) anger at her husband for taking her less seriously when she becomes a full-time wife and mother.

But while both the lower- and upper-middle-class women could identify with Hope's struggles, there were some class differences in their sense of the options available to Hope. Lower-middle-class women tended to feel that Hope was extremely lucky, and that her frustration was in a sense misplaced, because they believed she could fulfill herself with other activities. Upper-middle-class women, on the other hand, tended to have more empathy for Hope's loss of self-worth and felt that even with her options she was in a bind between wanting to work and wanting to stay home. Thus, while upper-middle-class women could identify with Hope's dilemma of having *choices* and the anxiety of having to make a decision, lower-middle-class women felt that the very option of having different choices made Hope responsible for her own happiness. In order to flesh out some of the differences between the two groups of women, it may be helpful to look at the different groups in more detail.

Lower-Middle-Class Women's Reactions to Hope

Many women who came from a lower-middle-class background were sensitive to and identified with Hope's sense of frustration at having to choose between having a fulfilling family life and pursuing a career full time, but some found her annoying. One woman is Cindy (all names used are fictional), who was twenty-six years old, had been married for three years, and came from an Irish and Italian ethnic background. Cindy worked full time as an administrative assistant at a brokerage firm and was a college graduate. She described herself as coming from a working-class family in Bay Ridge; her mother and grandmother worked full time as waitresses. Her husband was a supervisor of phone clerks at a commodities trading firm, and their combined income was $55,000, which raised them to the middle class in terms of her present status.

Cindy began her interview by discussing her own plans whether to have children or not:

> I guess I'm gonna have to have a kid! Someday I guess I'm gonna do it. The way I'm looking at it I have at least four years 'cause I'm twenty-six, and you can have your first kid when you're forty now, so I'm not rushing. Like I want to have children but I don't want to mess everything else up, so I'm kind of putting that on hold. I want to buy a house first. . . . I don't want to have more than two children and I'd like to do that but at the same time have a career. (transcript no. 9)

When asked what she thought about the character of Hope, Cindy explained that she thought Hope was a frustrated person because she was stuck at home all day and did not have a fulfilling career. Attempting to explain the source of Hope's unhappiness with staying at home, Cindy compared Hope to her own sister-in-law, who also stayed at home:

> God, I hope I'm not like Hope! Because she's too dull. And she worries too much. See, this what I think like happens. Like my husband's sister is like this. Like she'll talk to me on the phone about something that doesn't seem important. But it's so important because she's home all day and she has nothing more important to

> think about and that's what Hope is like. That's definitely what she's like. She'll worry about something that's not really important to anybody else in the world but it's important to her 'cause she has nothing else more important to think of. She started to get more interesting when she started to go back to work and then she had another kid and she lost the interest. 'Cause she started to worry about little tiny things. (transcript no. 9)

For Cindy, the secondary female character Susannah was the ideal woman because she was perceived as being able successfully to combine work and family. As for many of the other women I spoke with from lower-middle-class backgrounds, staying at home represented for Cindy a closing off of the world. Unlike the upper-middle-class women, Cindy did not appreciate the "mandate of smallness" that *thirtysomething*'s creators self-consciously tried to construct and that many of the upper-middle-class women appreciated.

In general, many of the lower-middle-class women were able to understand the sources of Hope's frustration as stemming from being at home when she wanted to go back to work. This frustration was also tied to the fact that, of the two partners in the marriage, Hope was perceived as the one who had to make the compromises to make the marriage work, including staying at home. One woman in her forties, Adrienne, who had been born in Brooklyn and was living on the South Shore of Staten Island, exemplified this attitude. White and Irish-Catholic, Adrienne was married to a retired policeman and had one daughter, who was twenty-one. She described herself as coming from a working-class home (her mother also worked as a waitress), although, because she came from a violent home, she was periodically placed in foster care. After staying home to raise her children, she had gone back to school and was trying to make it as an artist. When we began to talk about the characters on *thirtysomething*, Adrienne observed that Hope was being set up by the writers as the ideal woman. She felt the writers had "stacked the deck" in favor of Hope because she was the one who was willing to make the most compromises in her life for family peace:

> Hope is definitely their ideal woman, because she is surrendering; she is the one who's making the most compromises, I see. I think the family is very important but it somehow . . . in terms of unleashing our potential and working on fulfilling ourselves, that isn't in *thirtysomething*. Hope has to make a compromise. And I think that's the way it always is. Hope now is a person who's married and has one [baby] and one on the way, you know. Somebody once said, it's not

> the big things that get to you, it's the little things, like your car isn't working, who's gonna take the kids, the husband isn't home, it's just a matter of how much time do you have, what are your priorities. You know, you sort of get lost in it all. The women on the show are the ones who are making the compromises. (transcript no. 11)

Relating her own life to Hope's, Adrienne went on to express anger that it was always the woman who had to make the compromises in the family:

> I think it's [Hope's life] a little . . . I don't think anybody can have it all, but I don't think the compromise always has to come from the woman. You know, 'cause I've paid the price for that. That's not necessarily the larger thing, but you know at my own personal level that it always seems that these compromises always seem to come off in terms of the woman. I did not go back to work when my daughter went. (transcript no. 11)

Adrienne believed that, in some ways, she had already lived through Hope's "nightmare" of always being the one in the family who had to make the compromises to secure family peace, and in a sort of feminist pep talk urged Hope to forge ahead with her own goals:

> My nightmare is already realized. I became Hope. In other words, my husband wanted to go into this business, put all our personal assets into it, and I got sucked into it, and now I'm trying to get on my own keel, and it's very hard, I can tell you I'm scared to death. Scared to death of going back to school now . . . I'm also Hope's sister, and I'm telling her, don't compromise. I can't say, throw the bum out, because he certainly is much more open than my husband ever was. Now of course my husband is changing, so it's going to be even hairier for Hope. (transcript no. 11)

Upper-Middle-Class Women's Reactions to Hope

Like their counterparts from lower-middle-class backgrounds, the upper-middle-class women I spoke with found Hope's conflicts over work and family to be "true to life." But they were more sympathetic to her compromises. Many of them identified especially with Hope's loss of self-esteem when she made the decision to stay home rather than work full time. They empathized with Hope's frustration at not being taken seriously by the outside world because she stayed home all day to take care of her children and her conflicts in adjusting to her new and devalued role as a wife and mother. This identification with Hope's frustration at losing her self-esteem was articulated not only by the women who had already confronted the same life choices but by single women in their thirties as well. These women could imagine feeling the same kinds of frustration in losing their sense of confidence when they fulfilled their traditional roles as wives and mothers in a society which devalues these roles.

An example of this attitude is Grace, who was thirty-one and single and who described herself as coming from an upper-middle-class family from Georgia. Her mother worked full time as a school administrator and her father was an executive in a Fortune 500 company. She was currently working full time in Manhattan as an executive secretary and had aspirations to being a dancer. Her income, including overtime, was $50,000. While Grace had had some relationships in college, she had not had a serious relationship throughout her twenties. Instead, her commitments had been to furthering her dance career, and all the money she earned went toward dance lessons. In thinking about her own life, Grace explained to me the difficulties she had had in trying to combine a commitment to her career and finding a man with whom she could build a family and who would be supportive of her career endeavors:

> I would like to be married if I was in a good relationship with somebody, but I just think that's unlikely that I'll meet somebody and have the kind of relationship that I want to have and have children and that sort of thing and still be able to pursue the career goals that I want to pursue . . . I don't know if the reason I haven't gotten married is because I haven't found somebody who's like that, or it's impossible to meet somebody like that so I don't end up in a relationship like that. I would never abandon my professional goals just to be married or have a family. (transcript no. 7)

Grace believed that in her own life, if she chose a husband over her career, she would feel a great deal of anxiety that she had not been able to pursue her dream, and she believed that Hope was probably suffering from a similar sense of frustration. More interestingly, Grace also felt that Hope's anger was inevitably tied to not being taken seriously, either by her husband or by the outside world, precisely because she had decided to be home full time with her child.

Grace referred to a specific episode to illustrate her point, one where Hope, then eight and a half months pregnant, decides to interview for a job in Washington, DC even though she lives in Philadelphia. Although she wants the job, Hope eventually decides not to take it because Michael feels that it will be too disruptive of their lives. Commenting on this episode, Grace went on to observe:

> I think it [the show] implies that if you have a need to work and you're not meeting or satisfying those needs, you're gonna be unhappy . . . It said that she [Hope] was frustrated at not being in a better position to take the job but probably she was more frustrated because she wasn't being taken seriously, and she really was giving up more than Michael was as far as a career went. (transcript no. 7)

Grace believed that, in order to have a marriage work, she might have to make similar compromises, and she envisioned having similar feelings of anger and frustration at having to be the one to make all the compromises. Although she wished that the writers of *thirtysomething* had provided an alternative scenario for Hope, Grace ultimately felt that the show did portray what happens in real life, where the woman is often forced to choose between career and family.[2]

What is most interesting about this reading is that Grace herself was resigned to having a career but no marriage, but recognized the inevitability of Hope's choice of family over career. The point is that many of the women found it plausible that a woman would choose her family over her career and that a man's career would come first. Even though Hope's decision to remain at home seemed plausible to most women, furthermore, this does not mean that in their own lives, particularly for the single women, they would give up the goal of having a fulfilling career and marriage. In fact, one of the saddest aspects of many of these interviews was the wish fulfillment expressed about having precisely these dual goals realized. As Grace reflected at another point:

> Having it all for me would be being involved in a really fulfilling, meaningful relationship and having a family life and having an interesting career and having enough money and health to do all that easily, and I think that that's totally possible. And I think that there are people who have it in real life. (transcript no. 7)

In Grace's case, being single and struggling to support herself would seem to contradict her cheerful thesis that it is "totally possible" to combine a successful career and family. At the same time, that lifestyle is held up as an ideal that she hopes to realize in her own life.

WOMEN'S PERCEPTIONS OF HOPE'S LIFE

Perhaps not surprisingly, although both groups of women could describe the pitfalls associated with playing out a traditional role in the family, when they were asked which female character's life they would like to have, the majority of women from both groups picked Hope. For example, Debbie, a thirty-one-year-old single woman who lived in Manhattan and was working as a word processor earning over $40,000 a year, offered this explanation for why Hope's life seemed so enviable:

> At the outset I love her house, except for the one wall by their bed because it's not finished, but besides that I love their house. I think she's got a good relationship, she's got a kid—I wouldn't mind having kids you know. She does a good job with them. She's got a great husband, I think he's terrific, nice looking, it looks like they have a good sex life. She's very pretty, he's very handsome, they're just very attractive. (transcript no. 13)

Interestingly enough, Debbie felt that Hope had the most enviable life, despite the fact that the same traditional division of labor had had deleterious effects on her own mother. Her father was a successful businessman who owned his own shoe business, and her mother stayed home and took care of the three daughters. Describing her background, she offered:

> You know, my mother basically did take care of everything. It was also part of her nature. She was a bit of a martyr and she's not . . . she's "no, no, I'll take the small piece," that type of thing. And I think it has really hurt her through the years because she wasn't able to express herself fully and it caused problems. She was into alcohol for a while . . . my father is the rule of the house and what he says goes, basically, so I wouldn't want to be that way. (transcript no. 13)

Even though Debbie's own mother had suffered, she saw no conflict between not wanting to be like her mother and wanting to have Hope's life. She felt that Hope and Michael had much more equality in their house and communicated better as a couple. Debbie was looking forward to being married to her boyfriend and to going back to school to become an interpreter for the deaf. She was worried, however, about her boyfriend's ability to support her because he was a struggling actor:

> Just yesterday, I was thinking about the fact that part of my nervousness in my relationship now is that my boyfriend is not the type . . . I

> mean he's very nurturing and caring, but he's not in a position financially to take care of me and he . . . we are very equal in helping each other make new decisions, but part of me wants a caretaker that will make decisions for me. I know that now, just yesterday, it sort of crystallized in my head and that scares me, because I want an equal relationship but part of me definitely wants to be taken care of. I always think somebody else will do it for me or decide for me or, you know, move my life along which isn't what's happening. (transcript no. 13)

In Debbie's case, then, part of what appeals to her about Hope's and Michael's life is the fact that, as a man who earns a high, steady income, Michael is indeed in a position to "take care of" Hope. Like many other women I spoke with in both the lower and upper middle class, Debbie expressed a desire not to have the kind of financial pressure that she felt with a boyfriend who could not be the primary breadwinner; in addition, as she acknowledged, she was socialized to think a man would protect her, financially and otherwise. Even for upper-middle-class women, then, part of the appeal of Hope's life is the fantasy of not having to share the role of breadwinner. In today's economy, as many women pointed out, even if the husband is earning a good living, a woman's income is often necessary in order for them to lead a middle-class lifestyle. For these and other reasons, then, the majority of women chose Hope's life as the most enviable.[3]

Focusing on what Hope does have, more generally, seemed to be a major theme among many of these women, so much so that some envisioned Hope's life as an ideal life for their daughters. One such woman is Arlene, an upper-middle-class Jewish woman from Princeton, New Jersey, a wealthy suburb where the Ivy League school is also located. After having a professional life in "the city," Arlene married somewhat late in life and decided to stay home full time with her son. Observing Hope's life, Arlene pointed out:

> If I had a daughter I would like to see her have a secure life with someone who really loves her, Hope's life! A husband who will take care of her, so she won't have to be alone. (transcript no. 4)

Women who described themselves as lower middle class also tended to cite Hope's life as the most enviable, and it was clear that her economic advantages as an upper-middle-class woman contributed to their choice. In fact, they often expressed resentment at Hope precisely because of the privileges that they believed she enjoyed as a result of her class. Adrienne explicitly mentioned Hope's class background as giving her a number of opportunities that she felt she did not have in her own life:

> I have to tell you honestly, I'm coming from a blue collar background she . . . the way Hope strikes me, I'm a bit envious. These women, they have families that can afford to send them to college and they can afford to live, things are sort of set for them and I sort of have that feeling like with Hope. In other words, so their place isn't finished, and there's a difference between not having a place finished and scrambling around to get food and pay the rent. Although I think she's a nice person. (transcript no. 11)

Some lower-middle-class women did not like Hope because they perceived her as not being appreciative enough of all the advantages she had. This was the case even when they were able to understand her conflicts over work and family. One young woman I spoke with, Antoinette, an eighteen-year-old from the Flatbush section of Brooklyn who was half Italian and half Puerto Rican, echoed this sentiment very strongly. She described herself as having come from a family background where drugs, alcohol, violence, and divorce were prevalent from an early age. After spending part of her youth in New Mexico, where her mother had moved after coming out as a lesbian, Antoinette returned to New York, where she was currently living with her mother's relatives, a middle-class Italian family from Flatbush, and working on her undergraduate degree. Thinking about the character of Hope, Antoinette offered the following observation:

> The one with dark brown hair, the passive one, Hope, married to the tall handsome guy, when I saw her, I saw a woman with a lot of things she wasn't appreciating. Like to me, I saw those things as like desirable things. She had a husband who was sensitive, like to tell you the truth, I do not like an over-sensitive male. . . . He's moderate. He's not oversensitive, but he's not like macho, and I see her with a child and a nice house and too nice, as far as I'm concerned that's a waste of money, but in the episode I watched last night, the father was taking off the coat for the little girl at the end and that was really touching to me, you know, and wanted to hear about her day. To me, I think she has a nice life and nothing to complain about. (transcript no. 12)

Antoinette believed that Hope was ultimately responsible for her own happiness and that her dissatisfaction was a result of her own inability to make her life interesting within the confines of a traditional role as wife and mother. As she explained:

> See, to me, that to have a healthy child and a husband who's there and that to me, you have nothing to complain about. As far as your own fulfillment, that's something you need to do on your own. She could take a course, she could get a sitter for three hours. She could get a part time job, even. I don't have any objection to leaving a child alone for four, five hours a day. That's essential to the child's development as well. I don't think she has anything to complain about. She's very close to having it all, except for the fact that she doesn't feel she has it all. But if that were me, I would be very content and very comfortable. (transcript no. 12)

Cindy was also puzzled by Hope's questioning of her life. She believed that Hope had a nice husband for whom she should be grateful, rather than criticizing. In describing why her own husband does not watch the show, Cindy explained that he was not very expressive when it came to talking about his feelings:

> He'll talk about other things. He doesn't like it [the show] because they're all talking about their feelings and . . . I don't know, all he ever says is, "It's stupid, it's stupid, how could you watch it?" My husband is like, "Why talk about it?" Maybe he thinks that it's like unimportant stuff so why talk about it. But he watches it with me sometimes even though he says that he hates it, even though he tells everybody he hates it. (transcript no. 9)

Contrasted with this view of her own husband as being inexpressive, Cindy offered the following critique of Hope for not appreciating what a nice husband she had:

> Hope makes me sick sometimes too. Because she's like so . . . the last show that I watched was when she went to her mother's anniversary party and she just made me sick. It's like why is she like fighting with him [Michael]?. I didn't know why she was fighting with him. He just seems so nice all the time. And she just seems like really bitchy. (transcript no. 9)

Some lower-middle-class women, then, tended to place the blame for Hope's dissatisfaction on herself for having made certain traditional choices and then not being happy with them. Michael, on the other hand, was lauded for accepting his responsibility as the breadwinner and was viewed as sympathetic even when he was ignoring Hope to pay attention to his job as provider for the family. As Cindy explained when asked to speculate on the reasons for Hope's dissatisfaction:

> 'Cause I think she's bored maybe, cause she wasn't working. She was having another kid. But like she decided to do that, she wanted to do that, so she did it. She was mad at him [Michael] because she felt like he wasn't giving her enough attention "cause he had to worry about his job. He *has* to worry about his job! She was out to here [pregnant], what does she want? And it upset me at the end. They just like looked at each other and she starts crying and I cry really easily so I was crying. It was sad. (transcript no. 9)

Interestingly enough, once Hope began seriously to question her role and openly challenge her position in the family, some lower-middle-class women began to perceive her character even more negatively, believing she had become "bitchy," selfish, and judgmental. Rather than sympathize with her struggles to break out of her maternal role as wife and mother, many women interpreted this as losing her "good" qualities.

One woman who felt this way was Michelle, who came from a traditional Italian family in the Graves End section of Brooklyn and who was currently living in Carnarsie. Michelle was twenty-one at the time of the interview and going to school full time at Brooklyn College (the first one in her family to go to college). She was planning on getting a master's degree in industrial psychology. She was also working as a file clerk at a law firm in Wall Street. She said she wanted to wait till her mid-thirties before having children. Thinking about her family background and the choices the women in her family had made with regard to work, Michelle offered the following description of herself in relation to these women:

> I'm definitely not traditional. I mean coming from an Italian family, traditional is you graduate from high school and you get married. And you don't even use that high school diploma you have. I mean you educate yourself and then you just get married and have children and that's what every woman in my family did, even in this day and age . . . I know I didn't like too much what I was seeing with the women in my family. I don't like the way they deal with things. They're supposed to be the caretakers and they have to depend on a man's salary, and I don't like it. (transcript no. 3)

Nonetheless, Michelle was critical of Hope for deviating from her own "nurturing" role in the family:

> Hope used to be my favorite, but not anymore. I think that she's changed a lot. She once played a very supportive role. She was supportive of everyone. And now I see her as sort of cynical to everyone. She finds fault with everyone now and she's very judgmental and very critical. (transcript no. 3)

Michelle perceived Melissa as her ideal character because she seemed able to combine the maternal qualities Hope was losing with an independent spirit:

> Of anyone, I think Melissa is the coolest one, so she would be pretty much close to a favorite. I think she's very independent and spunky. She listens to all the other characters. She listens to them and she tells them whatever's on her mind, regardless of who they are to her, whether it's a cousin or a friend or if she holds a close relationship with one of the characters or another, she won't favor that person. (transcript no. 3)

Summary

While the majority of the women could relate to Hope's conflicts, and were able to expound at length on the reasons Hope might be frustrated with her life, most lower- and upper-middle-class women would still choose her life. One way to address this contradiction is to look at the results of a fall 1990 *Time* magazine poll of 505 men and women between the ages of eighteen and twenty-four, in which four out of five respondents believed that it was difficult to juggle work and family and that too much pressure was placed on the woman to bear these burdens. Perhaps because of this belief in the difficulty women would find in juggling their roles, 51 percent of the female respondents put "having a long and happy marriage and raising well-adjusted children" ahead of career success (quoted in "Women: The Road Ahead" 1990:13).

In my own study of female viewers of *thirtysomething*, there also seemed to be a consensus that it was extremely difficult to juggle work and family successfully, and most thought that it was probably not possible for a woman to "have it all." Comparing the conflicts she believed *thirtysomething* was trying to portray with the lines of women she knew, Debbie explained:

> In real life, most of the people that I work with, the [women] lawyers, they don't have other lives, so I don't think it's ["thirtysomething"] unrealistic. Anybody that puts a lot of time into their career at a certain point is gonna have a strain in other areas of their lives. You can't "have it all" if "it all" has to mean everything, if you know what I mean. (transcript no. 13)

This belief was held by women who were currently juggling career and family, by women who were married but had no children, and by women who were single and had active careers—in short, by women at all different stages of the career/family life cycle. Even when women were in fact combining some form of work and family in their present lives, there seemed to be enough frustration with this situation that they believed it was difficult to combine an active work and family life successfully.

Interestingly enough, no one questioned the idea that men could achieve some kind of reasonable balance. Michael, for example, though working hard at his advertising agency, is also shown cheerfully doing such domestic chores as feeding the baby, cooking, and playing with the baby. At the same time, we also get to watch him play in high level power games at his job at an advertising agency. Elliot, too, not only gets to "play" at work, that is, have a creative job thinking up catchy advertising slogans, he also gets to be involved in his children's lives, seeing them in school performances, teaching them games, watching television with them. The men, in other words, lead those very lives from which the women on the show are excluded. And, rather than balking at the injustice of men being able to have it all, women viewers seem to accept this "gender boundary."

Given this perception that it is difficult, if not impossible, for most working women also to have a completely satisfying home and family life, many women opted for Hope's life, feeling that it seemed to offer more *emotional* fulfillment than the single career women on the show seemed to have. For, having set up a dichotomy of work versus family by having the career women on the show be single and the married women on the show stay home full time, *thirtysomething* reinforces the idea that it is indeed *not* possible for a woman to "have it all." Therefore, viewers saw Hope as having the closest approximation of having a happy life in having attained a successful *family* life, even though she had to compromise on her desire for an active work life. As Debbie summed it up:

> I think Hope is mostly happy except for certain issues. Is anyone ever happy all the time? Like happy with everything, you know. I don't

> ever expect to be happy with everything all the time. Also, I don't think there's anybody who doesn't realize that everything in life is a compromise to a certain degree. I mean when you have kids there are times when you wish you didn't have kids for whatever reasons, whether it's because you want to go out or you want to have a career. (transcript no. 13)

More generally, given the choices on the show between being a woman who has a family but no work life and being a woman with a work life but no family, most of the women would choose Hope's life, despite its frustrations. As Michelle said:

> But they also tell you that it's good to have a career, but at the same time it's more important to have a family, because they show you the perfect one is Hope, they show you how she has a family, she's an excellent mother and she's a very good wife, and at the same time she's very intelligent. (transcript no. 3)

Given this reality, we can perhaps also read the choice of Hope's life as a cultural ideal and fantasy for women in this era. That many of the women acknowledged that they might not be happy with Hope's life even if they had it only highlights the degree of unhappiness and dissatisfaction that these women felt with their current arrangements. These arrangements were unsatisfactory precisely because they left women with the sense of falling behind in one realm or the other, as they struggled to keep afloat in a sea of clashing goals and expectations.

What this ultimately suggests is that if the era during which these women grew up was characterized by "great expectations" for women, the post-feminist era may instead be thought of as an era of increasingly diminished expectations. These lowered expectations, in turn, suggest that women are discouraged not only about the possibility of attaining a successful work and family life but about achieving *any* kind of reasonable balance between the two.

Melissa: Reactions to Being Single

Of all the female characters on *thirtysomething*, Melissa elicited the broadest range of reactions from the female viewers. This relatively wider range of responses seemed to hinge on her status as a single woman. Women appeared to emphasize different aspects of her life, depending on their own contradictory feelings about what it means to have a career but no family. These contradictory feelings were expressed by both lower- and upper-middle-class women, single and married women, younger and older women. Moira, a twenty-nine-year-old Jewish school teacher from Park Slope, was married with no children. She came from a middle-class background, growing up in a large apartment in Queens, New York. Bright, funny, and well-educated, Moira expressed the ambivalent feelings many of the women had toward Melissa:

> I like Melissa, except when I don't. She is aware of the irony in many situations. She is funny and sarcastic. In some ways, like clothes and career choices, she is very contemporary, but her Jewish roots always tug at her. She cannot entirely rid herself of those ideals and expectations. I like that she is always aware of this struggle. (questionnaire no. 15)

In general, however, women's reactions did break down somewhat along class lines, with many lower-middle-class women feeling basically negative about Melissa as a character. Although they sympathized with her plight as a single woman, they believed that she was basically responsible for her situation, since her class privilege led her to focus more energy on being an artist than on "settling" down and finding a husband. Other lower-middle-class women felt more positively about Melissa, and spoke in envious terms about her class privileges, which allowed her to pursue a number of different tracks. These women reacted positively to Melissa's perceived independence from convention, and expressed a similar desire to be able to go into uncharted territory. Unfortunately, their own class location precluded their ability to make the same life choices as Melissa, and thus many of them were left to admire from afar Melissa's "eccentric" pursuit of a nonconventional career and lifestyle.

Upper-middle-class women, on the other hand, believed that Melissa was much more like them, in the situations she confronted and the language she used to describe her life. In addition, many upper-middle-class women could construct Melissa as a positive figure whose single status allowed her many options that a married person might otherwise not have. In order to demonstrate how Melissa's character elicited a broad range of responses, it may be helpful to turn directly to viewers' reactions.

Lower-Middle-Class Evaluations of Melissa's Life

Many lower-middle-class women had a primarily negative evaluation of Melissa as a person. This dislike, in turn, seemed to stem from their belief that Melissa was responsible for her single status, that she was too "flighty," "immature," and "unstable" to make the kind of commitment necessary to have a relationship. Many women felt that Melissa embodied a whole host of traits that they had defined their own life in opposition to: instability, impermanence, not being "settled down," and so on. By projecting these negative characteristics onto Melissa, these women were able to affirm their own feelings about what *is* necessary to be happy in life, namely, to be able to "focus" on one thing and to know yourself.

For example, Antoinette, the eighteen-year-old from Flatbush, believed that Melissa's life was completely unstable. She began by describing Melissa as "typical of a New York City, I don't have a husband, and I'm gonna be an artist" type. Echoing other lower-middle-class women's assessments, Antoinette distanced herself from this kind of "yuppie" who did not take the time to try to meet men and instead selfishly focused on her own needs. In her view, Melissa was responsible for her unhappiness because she aspired to be different from other people and did not spend enough time going after those things, including a home and children, that would give her more permanence in her life.

This negative view of Melissa was echoed by many lower- middle-class women, who also believed that Melissa's privileged class background gave her the luxury to pursue her own interests, whether or not those interests would give her any security. For these women, however, Melissa was ill served by her class privilege in that she was left wanting everything but having no ability to focus on any one thing. As Antoinette pointed out:

> I find Melissa to be too flighty and wanting too much, not knowing, you can't search for something if you don't know what you want and you can't say that there's no men out there, if you don't know what kind you are even looking for, you know. So I think her trauma is brought on by herself and I see her more as like somebody who would never be satisfied. I know what I want is maybe hard to get but I know that I will be satisfied when I get it. But there's people who are always looking but then you get the feeling that even if they got exactly what they wanted, they're not happy with themselves. I don't think she's happy with herself. I don't think she's content with herself. I think if she were content with herself she could be content with somebody else. Like if you don't like yourself, you don't like a lot of other people. (transcript no. 12)

Here Antoinette raises the issue of Melissa's happiness in terms of her inability to be satisfied with anything in her life. Many lower-middle-class women viewed Melissa negatively precisely because she did not realize the value of what she did have and instead complained endlessly about everything she did not have. Thus while many of these viewers identified with her wish to find a good man, or to get a career going, her class position as a privileged woman from a wealthy family led many lower-middle-class women to criticize her for her insistence on verbalizing her unhappiness. These women felt it was important to keep a sense of perspective and to take responsiblity for making one's life secure. This perhaps makes sense, since lower-middle-class women felt that they had no other choice but to figure out how to make their own lives secure economically, since there was no privileged class background to shield them from economic downturns.

Not all lower-middle-class women viewed Melissa with such hostility. In fact, some lower-middle-class women cited her approvingly, and this approval was related to the kind of life she was able to live, precisely because of her class status. For example, Stacie, a thirty-five-year-old registered nurse and mother of three boys who had been in therapy and was in an unhappy marriage, gave the following assessment of Melissa:

> She's great. She believes in her own style and tough on anyone who doesn't like it. I like her roll with the punch attitude and go get 'em determination. (questionnaire no. 8)

Stacie was able to enjoy Melissa precisely because she believed that Melissa was able to assert who she was, despite what other people thought. This "roll with the punch" attitude could be linked, in turn, to her relatively privileged class status, which might cushion her from any blows, psychic or material, received because of her attitude. In other words, Melissa was able to believe in herself and let things roll off of her because she was given a secure economic (and psychical) base from which she could go out into the world, trusting that she could weather any difficulties that might come her way. For many women, Melissa was a kind of role model. Susan, a lower-middle-class, forty-eight-year-old office manager and mother of two, offered:

> I admire her individuality and courage to be different; she's a free spirit, fun, adventuresome, always ready to take a chance, act on instinct, good with children, needs to find someone who isn't afraid of a woman who is strong. (questionnaire no. 3)

Melissa seemed to invite admiration from many lower-middle-class women, then, because she was able to live the kind of life that they wished they could lead, had they had the same economic resources to "take a chance and act on instinct." For example, Adrienne, the South Shore woman who was returning to school after raising her children, gave the following account of why Melissa was the one she liked best:

> Because she's [Melissa] the one who I would like to be. She's the photographer and that's how I'd like to be. 'Cause I'm an artist and I've never had the space to fully work on that . . . not so much that she's young, but in other words, I just like that scene, she has her studio . . . and she is a bit of an eccentric and you know, so far, I don't have the nerve to be that eccentric. (transcript no. 11)

Like their counterparts who did not like Melissa, however, all too often these women had continually to stake out the secure route in order to be able to survive in a perilous world. This push toward security, in turn, left little if any room to deviate or be "eccentric." Thus, like those who didn't like Melissa, these women felt that Melissa's class status afforded her opportunities not only materially but, perhaps even more crucially, *emotionally* to depart from the straight and narrow path. Whereas some lower-middle-class women judged this deviation harshly, and felt Melissa was responsible for making some mid-course correction to "straighten out" her life and find a man, others looked enviously at a life that did not have to adhere so rigidly to a secure path.

Upper-Middle-Class Women's Evaluations of Melissa's Life

In general, upper-middle-class women were much more sympathetic to Melissa as a person. Like their-lower-middle-class counterparts, these women identified with Melissa's plight as a single woman. But unlike the lower-middle-class women, they did not blame Melissa for her single status, instead seeing her as part of a larger historical problem of too many single women and not enough good men.

For example, many of the upper-middle-class women felt that, while they envied certain aspects of Melissa's life, they basically pitied her. For these women, being single was not an enviable state but rather something to be endured before "Mr. Right" came along. As Arlene, the full-time mother from Princeton, explained:

> In terms of relating, well, going back to when I was single, I think I could relate to Melissa, 'cause I lived in the city for about four or five years, from twenty-nine to thirty-four. I got married later in life. I was a real late bloomer, so I did a lot of traveling in my early twenties. Then I got my own apartment in Murray Hill and I really did the

> whole thing and the going to clubs, and dating, and here I am. At thirty-four I got married. I met my husband in an after hours club. But I was a real late bloomer, there was no way at twenty-four, twenty-five, twenty-six I was ready to settle down. I could relate to Melissa at that time of my life, the loneliness and dating. (transcript no. 4)

Many women tended to project their own ambivalent feelings about being single onto Melissa, so that, while they could admire her independence, they nevertheless felt that, for themselves, being single was a depressing and lonely experience. One young woman, Judy, a twenty-four-year-old elementary school teacher who was herself single, cited both Hope and Melissa as her favorite characters. In attempting to account for why she liked Melissa, she offered the following assessment:

> I like Melissa because she is an interesting character. She is artistic, funny, and single- although she wants to be in a relationship. I would like her as a friend. She is caring and reliable . . . I wouldn't want to deal with Melissa's loneliness, although I admire her independence. (questionnaire no. 12)

For those upper-middle-class women who enjoyed the character of Melissa and her life, being single was not perceived as completely onerous, but had desirable aspects to it as well. These positive aspects included having a relatively greater degree of freedom of movement; being more of one's own person; having an interesting career; being a good friend to others outside a strictly defined nuclear unit; and retaining one's individuality, "spunkiness." One woman named Jane, for example, a twenty-six-year-old lawyer in a prestigious law firm, offered the following account of why she enjoyed Melissa as a character:

> I think of my former days. I was an actress and so I have this really weird, artsy side to me and that part of me identifies with her [Melissa] 'cause she's pretty free wheeling and what she does is very creative and that's what I did for a long time till I came here. I went to Performing Arts High School and then I was going to be an actress until I decided I was going to be a lawyer. (transcript no. 14)

This ability to be unconventional was explicitly related to Melissa's condition of being single; she could be her own person, in other words, in part because she was not in a relationship where she would be defined as a girlfriend, wife, or mother. In this sense, being single was not viewed as a lonely and isolating experience but rather as an *opportu-*

nity for women to assert their own identities outside any fixed societal definitions.

In fact, the women who were perhaps best able to articulate this sense of Melissa as being able to retain her own identity were those women who, because of their own sexual preferences for other women, had already long ago abandoned an identity based on a heterosexual union with a man. One woman, Marita, a bisexual woman in her mid-thirties, with one child, who had a Ph.D. and a university post, offered the following description of Melissa precisely in terms of this idea that Melissa stands outside traditional relationships to a husband or child:

> I'm always surrounded by people like the photographer [Melissa], all of my friends are like her, crazy, obnoxious, wild, artistic, creative . . . I think the single photographer [Melissa], she is the strongest woman in the whole show, among the women, and she's single, has no children. And that's the way it is in society. The single woman in her thirties with no children is the professional woman, is the strong woman, all the other ones are caught with the children, with the husband, even if they are professional. As soon as one of the criteria, like being a wife or having a child, they take over somehow, even if they are professional, you know, so I think it's real, it's realistic. (transcript no. 5)

Another woman, Amelia, a forty-six-year-old lesbian, also with one child, who works as a media designer and earns approximately $50,000 (which gives her and her psychotherapist lover a combined income of $90,000), also offered the following assessment of Melissa as being able to "struggle" with issues outside men and family:

> I don't want any of their lives. They're all too terminally straight for me. But if I translate it into a world I could live in, I guess it would be Melissa- at least she has a job I can relate to and some sense of an existential struggle that doesn't revolve around men and family. (questionnaire no. 13)

In sum, whether they liked the character of Melissa or not, the upper-middle-class women who participated in my study had strong reactions to her status as a single person. Many women believed that, in their own lives, being single was a lonely and desperate affair, and they in turn projected these feelings onto Melissa. As Rhoda, a married, full-time mother from Princeton, summed it up:

> But on the show they portray Melissa as really wanting what the other people have, she wants to get married. Especially women over thirty, everyone complains about the single scene, everybody hates it. (transcript no. 4)

Other women did not view Melissa's status as a single person as undesirable and instead tended to emphasize the positive aspects, including the ability to retain a more independent lifestyle, to maintain strong friendships, to follow one's own path in life, and so on. Some younger women especially idealized Melissa's life, and focused on such things as her unconventionality, her young boyfriend, even her apartment, as enviable aspects of her life. Still other women felt ambivalent about Melissa's single status, and their answers reflected this ambivalence.

Reactions to Ellyn

By and large, both lower- and upper-middle-class women had the most negative reactions to the character of Ellyn, the "career woman" on the show, who is often portrayed as screwing up in her love life. The negative reactions that viewers had seemed to hinge on three following issues: their discomfort with the way she handled herself with men; her insecurity and lack of direction in life; and her overemphasis on her career.

It is interesting that upper-middle-class women had a lot less tolerance for Ellyn's verbalizing of her anxieties (unlike that of the other female characters on *thirtysomething*) even when they could imagine themselves in a similar situation. While lower-middle-class women saw Ellyn as a relatively privileged woman who was neurotic and annoying, upper-middle-class women characterized her harshly, in the angriest terms imaginable. In this sense, lower-middle-class women tended to have somewhat more charity towards Ellyn, even though they perceived her as a breed apart from themselves with her obsessive and neurotic tics. Upper-middle-class women, on the other hand, felt much more threatened by her personality, and were at pains to distance themselves from her at every opportunity. For upper-middle-class women, then, who may themselves be in high-powered careers, there seemed to be much more of a need to proclaim how different they were from Ellyn and how Ellyn was in fact to blame for her inability to have a satisfying home life. Thus, while both lower- and upper-middle-class women could relate to conflicts over having a successful home and work life, when it came to the character of Ellyn they both felt justified in blaming Ellyn's gender crisis on herself.

Perhaps most interesting was the finding that many upper- middle-class women expressed a great deal of criticism of how Ellyn was constructed as a character on *thirtysomething*. They were conscious that they were being fed a stereotype of a career woman, and many of them resented the writers' constructing women in this light. In part as a result of their upbringing as privileged white women who were raised to see themselves as having options, this group of upper-middle-class women were aware that there were other choices out there than the ones that Ellyn was making. Thus, while they could in a sense let themselves be swept up in the characters and storylines of *thirtysomething*, even when they were self-conscious of the constructed nature of television, when it came to the character of Ellyn, many upper-middle-class women protested long and loud about how unfair television was to portray women in this light.

Many of the upper-middle-class women in the study had a strong negative reaction to how Ellyn conducted herself in her relationships with men, particularly when she rejected a nice single male character in order to have an affair with a married man. As Leslie, a thirty-three-year-old mother from Park Slope who was working part time as a lawyer, offered:

> And I find the Ellyn character just excruciatingly annoying and ditzy and selfish and shallow. I mean it must be something about her character I would sort of be sympathetic towards a person who's got a good job and works in government and is committed to that—that's sort of laudable—but I don't like how she purposely got involved with a married man. (transcript no. 8)

Like other women I spoke with, Leslie felt that Ellyn was the embodiment of "smart woman, foolish choices," a type of woman who has cropped up on recent best-seller lists during this period who was somehow masochistic and sought out inappropriate and unavailable men. Debbie, the single word processor who was dating the actor, described Ellyn as follows:

> Ellyn—I don't know what she's looking for but she's looking in all the wrong places! Ellyn, Ellyn, Ellyn. I think she's just looking for someone to love her. I don't think she can even delineate anything further than that. I don't think she can look further than that

> because she wants to be loved so much. Her parents just broke up and I think she got a real fear of . . . you know so she chose a married man . . . because I think at the time she was afraid of something more accessible to her. But then she got involved. I don't really know what the story is, I don't thinks she knows what her story is. (transcript no. 13)

Other upper-middle-class women raised the issue of how male viewers perceived Ellyn as a partial justification for their own negative feelings toward her. As Arlene, the thirty-nine-year-old full-time mother from Princeton, pointed out:

> The guys don't like Ellyn. She's totally neurotic, she sabotages her relationships, she's whiny, afraid to commit, her sentences don't even come out. I never heard her once say on the show that "I would like to settle down, get married and have a child," whereas Melissa will say, "I want marriage" and "I want to make babies." Melissa's more mature. She's [Ellyn] more successful at work, but a complete failure at relationships. Her personal life is shit. (transcript no. 4)

Even when they were neutral about Ellyn as a character, these viewers were at pains to point out how they were completely unlike her, citing her overemphasis on her career as a reason why they could not relate to her. For example, Grace, the single word processor trying to pursue a career in the arts, invoked this seeming dichotomy between Ellyn's professional and personal life:

> I don't relate to Ellyn in any way. I see her as very traditional in her career goals, and I mean, she's actually gone after a real traditional career, she's going for some sort of nine to five job, and I see her as always putting her career first, regardless of any sort of human relationship and probably the most focused on her career of any of the women, just solely on her career. (transcript no. 7)

Grace saw Ellyn's pursuit of a traditional male path toward career and away from human relationships as following the wrong path and as implicitly offering a critique of women who follow the male model of achievement. This negative evaluation of women who take the "traditional" path toward achievement is in turn underscored through the portrayal of Ellyn as in fact not being able to have a successful personal life. This stereotype of the successful career woman was strongest in the first season of *thirtysomething* and was later modified or "softened."

However, it is interesting that Grace was able to draw the analogy between Ellyn and the stereotypical "career woman," suggesting that the terms of the show devalue women who pursue careers and valorize women who instead seek human relationships.

Many women in fact questioned the show's premise that a career woman could not have an active family life. Jane, the attorney, who was engaged to another attorney, described her confusion over why *thirtysomething* does not portray married women with active careers:

> I like Ellyn. I think she has her shit together pretty well. 'Cause she's a career woman and as much as she wants to meet someone I think she'll deal fairly well with her situation. I think the only true career women on the show is Ellyn or maybe Melissa, but they're single. It's kind of strange that there's not a married corporate woman there too. Maybe it's just not in that generation. But it should be. It's not that far removed from me. (transcript no. 14)

In Jane's own life, however, she saw some conflicts arising, in that her fiancé would want her to stay home and raise the kids. When asked how she was going to mediate between having an active career and children, she replied:

> I don't know yet. I have no idea. It's a concern for my relationship because my fiance is very traditional and wants someone who'll stay at home but I just can't foresee that for me. (transcript no. 14)

Many upper-middle-class viewers blamed the writers for making Ellyn so "messed up." These women felt that the writers were intentionally trying to make the single characters seem "less together" than the married ones. As Risa, a single, twenty-seven-year-old educational researcher from Park Slope, Brooklyn, pointed out:

> In general, I think they pick on the single female characters—they always have crummy things happening to them and they are portrayed as emotionally much less together. Ellyn in particular. The woman seems to be a basket case most of the time. She's flakey. (questionnaire no. 11)

Other women, too, echoed this dissatisfaction with the way Ellyn was portrayed. For example, Laura, a thirty-three-year-old lesbian woman from Park Slope, reacted strongly to Ellyn's character. Laura, who had grown up in an upper-middle-class family and was currently living with her commercial designer lover while she was trying to make it as a poet, had a strongly negative reaction to Ellyn's transformation from a person with some integrity to a "vamp":

> Ellyn was a character that I thought had a lot more integrity than I think they portray her now. I think her character is less and less appealing and that has to do with the fact that they put her into this role, they changed her role on the show to being this vampy type woman, I mean the way she dresses . . . the way that she sits with her psychiatrist, it's so unappealing and I don't think believable, they've distorted her character with a married man and all that crap when she was a fairly dynamic character in the beginning with a career and successful. They changed all that. (transcript no. 15)

Laura, like some of the other women I spoke with, believed that the writers on *thirtysomething* had no idea what career women were really about and chose to "punish" career women by making them neurotic in their personal lives. They believed that career women were often portrayed negatively in the media, and did not accept the terms of the dominant culture. For many others, however, Ellyn, rather than the writers, was perceived as somehow to blame for her character, and moral outrage was often heaped on her for being so "messed up in the head."

For example, many women felt that Ellyn embodied all the undesirable traits they had come to associate with the term "career woman": aggressiveness, pushiness, being over *and* undersexed. This was due to their belief that, in order to make it "in a man's world," career women like Ellyn had to become like men. Listen to Risa, the single educational researcher, describe Ellyn:

> And Ellyn is in that role that I dislike so much. That ball-busting corporate woman, like if you're not going to be a man in this man's world, you ain't gonna make it, and she's making it like a man. (transcript no. 10)

Other women also echoed this fear that one would have to compromise one's femininity to be successful in a career. As Jan, Risa's single, twenty-nine-year-old roommate, also explained:

> You know, they show you with Ellyn that you really can't have it all. You're compromising a lot of your own femininity if you do that and . . . what they are showing her is being in a workforce as a woman, but not having any sort of female, anything uniquely female 'cause she's in the workworld . . . She's just like a man, she's just behaving, she just plugged herself into this. (transcript no. 10)

More generally, there was the sense that career women, while not necessarily becoming like men, nevertheless lost their compassion as they became overly aggressive in trying to succeed. As Risa continued:

> I see people where I work that are much more like Ellyn than like anybody else on the show. They're just there and they're going to do their thing and they're going to impress everyone and they are out there with their career and it's like, give me a break. (transcript no. 10)

In general, many lower-middle-class women envied Ellyn for her ability to be strong-willed, but also felt that she could only be *truly* happy if she became less "messed up" and found the right man. This view was interesting because it expressed their desire not only to be able to have enough social power to speak up but, at the same time, to be able to inhabit more traditional roles for women. In their view, while it was important for women to have their own voice, there was still the sense that, in order to find life's true sources of happiness, one had to look beyond "careers" (which for most lower-middle-class women simply meant dead-end jobs) and toward the family.

For example, Cindy, the twenty-six-year-old administrative assistant from Bay Ridge, described why Ellyn was her least favorite character:

> I hate her because she just gets on my nerves sometimes too. I don't know, I like what she's doing with her life, but I don't like it that she's so messed up in her head . . . doesn't she see a psychiatrist or something? Didn't she have a nervous breakdown or something too? And what she did to that guy was terrible. The blond guy. He didn't do anything and she just flipped out. And I don't understand why she got rid of him. Do you know why? I don't know why. (transcript no. 9)

Other lower-middle-class women seemd to echo this assessment of Ellyn as not knowing what she wants from men, yet at the same time seeking "desperately" to define herself in relation to men. Ellyn was perceived as demonstrating two conflicting traits, both of which made her unappealing. On the one hand, she was viewed as a kind of masochistic throw-back to women who were desperate about men. Viewers reacted strongly to this kind of regressive femininity where the only way a woman can define herself is in relation to men. On the other hand, many lower-middle-class women also criticized to her overemphasis on her career, which indicated she was unable to create a stable personal life. They perceived her as a privileged woman, selfishly pursuing a career to get rich, without focusing on the non-materialistic things in life, like a home and family. These two traits—an overemphasis on a career coupled with a terrible personal life—were linked, furthermore, in many women's minds. That is, Ellyn's desperation with men was linked to her single-minded pursuit of a career. Beneath the veneer of the successful career woman lies a woman who is not only unlucky in love but is incapable of forming *any* kind of healthy emotional relationship.

In these commentaries, the fact that men might pursue these goals was never once questioned and there seemed to be an implicit assumption that to be a man is in fact to pursue these goals. There was no criticism, in other words, of men who behaved like Ellyn, but for a woman to act this way was to invite the strongest kinds of cultural censure. In addition, the men on the show who do pursue these goals at the same time have a seemingly rich and rewarding family life. This ability of men to "balance" work and family is never questioned. For the female characters to have these dual goals, however, was to raise the specter of being a failure in one realm or the other, as evidenced by the dichotomy of Ellyn as successful career woman/ personal failure.

What emerges most clearly from these lower-middle-class women's reactions to Ellyn is not only that there still exists a double standard but that women are considered deviant if they ignore their traditional spheres of competence. Men, on the other hand, will be lauded for having a career and, more importantly, can expect to have a satisfying home life as well.

This reaction is, in turn, related to their sense of career women as somehow a "breed apart" from them socially, like strange beings who are high-strung and incapable of having a normal life.

Conclusion

Perhaps the best way to describe women's reactions to the characters on *thirtysomething* is to raise Stuart Hall's (1981) original formulation of the concept of "preferred reading" in viewers' responses to popular culture. This concept refers to the idea that the texts of popular culture do in fact try to direct their readers toward one specific reading of their products. David Morley, in referring to this idea of a preferred reading, has also described it as a kind of "structured polysemy" (Morley 1993) wherein a text may have many meanings but does try to structure or prefer one set of meanings over another. This theory allows for the fact that there may be alternative, negotiated or oppositional, readings to the preferred reading of the text, but it is useful because it emphasizes that the text does in fact work to situate the reader so as to accept one set of meanings over another.

Where this study enters into this discussion, I believe, is to demonstrate the ways in which female viewers attempt to *contextualize* these preferred meanings within the terms of their own lives. In most cases, for example, the women in this study did not exercise a kind of "semiotic democracy" (Morley 1993:15) in order to routinely invent alternative or oppositional meanings to those offered by the creators of *thirtysomething*. Rather, for the most part, they chose to accept the preferred meanings that were offered about gender on the program. On the other hand, they continually transformed and transposed the events on the program into the warp and weft of their own life histories as women who were both constructed by and constructing their lived class experiences.

What this suggests is that the female viewers were arguably passive *and* active with respect to the texts of *thirtysomething*: passive in accepting the dominant hegemonic framework of the program, which chastised women for deviating too far from traditional gender roles, yet active in contextualizing these issues into the framework of their own lives. Using Ang's (1990) useful distinction between the terms "active" and "powerful," we may describe the female viewers as active in terms of their reading of *thirtysomething*, but probably something less than powerful with respect to their ability to define alternative scenarios to those set out by the program.

Perhaps what can be learned from these observations is that, while it is useful to study the texts of popular culture, to really understand the way cultural hegemony works it is necessary to engage in the micro-level research of ethnography to see how individuals actively incorporate dominant meanings into their lives. Through interviews with female viewers, we learned that *thirtysomething* was not effective because it simply imposed a dominant ideology onto a passive viewing public, but rather because it was *open* enough to invite each reader to identify with its characters and in this way engaged the reader enough to accept its preferred meanings about gender. A structural analysis of determinate meanings, then, as might be suggested by traditional psychoanalytic or marxist theories, could not have revealed the *reciprocal* relationship that viewers engaged in as they incorporated the meanings of *thirtysomething* into their own lives.

More generally, what is revealed by viewers' responses to *thirtysomething* is that ethnographic research cannot simply remain at the level of the individual, but must also look at how individual responses are themselves located within broader cultural frameworks. David Morley has described ethnography as concerned with "tracing the specifics of general, systemic processes—for instance, the particular tactics that various members of a given society have developed to make do with the cultural resources that society still offers them" (Morley 1993:18). Scholars such as Tamar Liebes and Elihu Katz (1990), who have looked at different viewing publics in Israel and America, for example, or Ellen Seiter and her colleagues, who have studied German viewers (1989), suggest that cultural meanings are specific and influence how a viewer will respond to a text.These findings suggest that even if viewers accept the preferred meaning of a text, it is necessary to see what that acceptance means in terms of the dominant culture they live in. Thus it is necessary continually to reflect on the social and cultural contexts viewers live within to understand what these preferred meanings *mean* to their specific lives.

Notes

1. For example, Debbie, an upper-middle class single woman, thirty-one, who was working full time as a word processor in Manhattan and who indicated that she would take time off to raise her children when she got married, offered the following assessment of Hope's life:

> Hope really hasn't had much of a chance to [be in the workworld]. . . . she's very busy at home and when she tried to put herself in the workworld it almost destroyed her relationship with Michael. Because first of all she had to put her things aside for Michael's career—there was a job that was offered to her in Washington and she went for it [the interview] simply to assert herself. In fact, saying "Why do I always have to put myself second to you?" "Why can't I explore this?" (transcript no. 13)

2. As Grace pointed out,

> She [Hope] realized it [not pursuing her career] was a realistic choice she would have to make at that point—she couldn't pursue the job in Washington and still have a relationship with Michael that she wanted to have and she did want the child and that would have caused complications. (transcript no. 7).

3.The only women I could locate in my sample who did not choose Hope's life were some women at either end of the age spectrum, that is, a few relatively younger women who thought Melissa's life looked like more "fun" and a few older women who envied Melissa's perceived

Chapter 5

Married with Children and Single White Females: *thirtysomething* Women Tell Their Stories

Thirtysomething was specifically tailored to mirror the lives of upper-middle-class married people in their thirties with children. This was the life situation of Marshall Herskovitz and Edward Zwick, the show's creators, and it was their explicit artistic mandate when creating the program. In addition, *thirtysomething* was created as an artistic answer to those domestic comedies of the 1950s that depicted married life as essentially tranquil and harmonious.[1] Unlike those shows, *thirtysomething* is ironic and self-conscious about married life, and presents characters who agonize out loud over the near-impossibility of keeping it all together—their marriage, their house, their careers, themselves—in the 1980s.

For the married women I spoke with, *thirtysomething* articulated many of the dilemmas they saw themselves facing in their own lives. Whether the issue was dividing up the homemaking and child care, dealing with feelings of overload from work and guilt over not spending enough time with their children, or finding time between family and work responsibilities to be sexually intimate with their husbands, many of the married women I spoke with felt that *thirtysomething* was chronicling their own lives. In this chapter we will see how two very different married women—Janice, an African-American woman originally from Jamaica, and Tamara, a white Jewish woman from Long Island—used *thirtysomething* to think through their choices over work and family.

Janice: "Being Selfish for Once"

In Chapter 4, we saw how women could relate to the life situations of the female characters of *thirtysomething*, even if they came from very different social and economic backgrounds. Janice typifies these women. Thirty-two at the time of the interview, Janice was a serious young woman who lived in the East New York section of Brooklyn, an overwhelmingly black neighborhood, where abandoned and run-down buildings are interspersed among residences, overall a far cry from the serene exurban landscapes of *thirtysomething*. She had immigrated from Kingston, Jamaica about eight years prior to our interview, and she periodically returned during summers to have her three children visit with relatives and generally to get them out of the city. Because she was concerned for her children's safety living in this section of the city, she was sending two of her children to a school run by her Anabaptist church. She and her husband, Robert, had a combined income (he was a cabdriver, she a nurse's aide) of about $40,000. Robert, also an immigrant from Jamaica, was both excited and resentful about her decision to go back to school. Describing his reaction to her schooling, she said:

> At this point my husband is totally spoiled. He can't understand why I don't come home to cook dinner, and I go and sit down with a book. I don't feel like that anymore, I don't want to have anything like my [domestic] work scheduled out for me anymore. If I feel to go and cook I go and cook, if I don't, I don't. (transcript no. 2)

In fact, Janice had dropped out of high school when she had her first child at the age of fifteen; so going to college represented a big step for her. Her own mother had worked her entire life as a school aide at various elementary schools in Jamaica, and Janice's grandmother had stayed home with her and her brothers and sisters. Janice, too, had stayed home while her children were young, and she was beginning to feel that if she did not make some changes in her life, she would end up as her mother and grandmother had done, poor and bitter about their life options. Unlike the majority of the women I interviewed, Janice was not a regular follower of *thirtysomething*. If anything, she liked to watch old movies. However, she would put it on when she wanted to relax after a long day of work and school. She began by recalling one particularly vivid episode for her, the one where Nancy and Elliot were getting separated. As she explained:

> I kind of liked that episode. I've seen other episodes which I haven't liked. I did not want to waste an hour—I have other things to do, like study and things like that. (transcript no. 2)

Because Janice was unlike the other women I interviewed, both because she was black and because she was not a "faithful" viewer, I thought it would be difficult at first to see how *thirtysomething* might relate to her life. As the interview continued, however, it soon became apparent that Janice did find relevance to this fictional world of upper-middle-class white people, precisely through the lens of gender. That is, whereas the class and race dimensions were clearly different between Janice and the fictional characters, as Janice herself was the first to point out, she found common ground in the conflicts that the female characters had. Describing her reaction to *thirtysomething*, for example, Janice recalled:

> *Thirtysomething* reminded me too much of real life! Because the same thing is going on in most people's lives—they're getting separated and the children are getting hurt. It reminds me too much of what is going on now. And the particular show I saw that evening, I thought maybe that could happen to me too. It reminded me of stuff that happens in my own life. Like the dialogue that passed back and forth between the husband and the wife. I don't like it when it's so close to home. (transcript no. 2)

When I asked Janice explicitly about how she could relate to a group of upper-middle-class white "yuppies," Janice offered the following explanation:

> The same thing happens for the poor, just the same. Because most of the time in the poor how what causes the problems is the financial problem, money, in the upper class it's still money because they want more than what they have. It's always money, one way or the other. It gets taken out in the relationship. . . . Also, most of the stuff between the husband and wife. They try to say things to hurt each other. We women, because men have it that we're the weaker sex, all we have for our defense are words, we say the most cruel things at times, because we have to get back at them. And you know that was what was happening on the show on the episode that I saw. (transcript no. 2)

Interestingly enough, Janice was able to relate to *thirtysomething* precisely in terms of where she was most different, that is, her income level. This is not to say that she did not recognize the difference in income levels, but rather that she believed fighting about money was a universal problem between men and women. In addition, Janice also related to the female partner's position as the "weaker sex." She believed that, as women, the characters tried to use whatever defenses they could. Thus, even though the women on *thirtysomething* had a lot more economic and social power than she did, Janice still identified with their position as women in a patriarchal society.

Janice's sense of a common tie with the female characters came through most poignantly when she described her own conflicts over work and family. Explaining why the characters Hope and Michael were arguing all the time, Janice drew a connection between Hope and herself as both wanting to put their own work first for once, and letting the family adjust to their new roles. Janice gave voice to a great degree of frustration, of having let years go by caring for others, and of wanting to be "selfish" for once in her life:

> I don't know if I'm being selfish but deep down inside I feel like it's just time for me. I've given the best years of my life to my husband and my children. And even though my children, they're not adult age where they can be on their own, I still think I should have something else for myself, because there's a lot of women who had children and went back to school right after. I stayed home most of their life, I did not leave them with babysitters, I was there for them twenty four hours, seven days. . . . When I saw my grandmother pass away, I was looking at her in the coffin, and I could remember all the years she had been there for her four children and for us. . . . She was a pleasant woman, and then she started to get so miserable and I wondered what it was in her life that made her so miserable all of a sudden. (transcript no. 2)

That Hope's situation as a privileged white woman who could choose whether to work or not would remind Janice of her black grandmother from Jamaica, a woman who had to raise two generations of children, at first seems implausible. For Janice, however, the connection was clear: living for others, as she perceived Hope and her grandmother as doing, could make one "miserable."

It is interesting, furthermore, that, as a lower-middle-class black woman, Janice did not simply fantasize about having a big house in the suburbs where she could stay home full time and not have to work, as theories that mass media serve as "compensatory" fantasies might suggest. I believe it is precisely her grandmother's experience, as well as her own life struggles, however, that opened Janice to the conflicted aspects of Hope's situation and gave her real entry into an otherwise distant narrative about yuppies.

Of course, it is possible that Janice's interest in *thirtysomething* is influenced by the desire that her life be as materially comfortable as that of those portrayed, but the more significant factors in her reading are the experiences she brings to it. Janice seems to derive from *thirtysomething* and her reflections on it a "lesson" that denying one's own goals inevitably leads to frustration. As a woman who had her first child at the age of fifteen, Janice is resentful at seeing her adolescence wrested away from her. Thus both her own and her grandmother's experience led Janice to relate to Hope's sense of frustration, rather than joy, at full-time mothering. Watching a television show about white upper-middle-class yuppies served as a vehicle for Janice to experience a whole range of emotions about trying to reconcile her own work and family life.

When I spoke with Janice six months after our initial interviews, she was still in school and working more hours as a nurse's aide, still focused on becoming a registered nurse. Her husband, while still complaining about not having hot cooked meals every night, had gotten used to her being in school and was grateful for the income her job provided. Her children, she reported, had adapted well to her new life, enjoying not only the extra clothing and games that her income generated for the family but the sense that their mother was becoming a "professional." For Janice, then, the message of *thirtysomething* was that it is important for women to work. As an immigrant who saw the women in her family suffer from lack of opportunities, Janice believed that working full time was the best way to realize her dreams.

Like many of the women I spoke with, Janice saw her own life as an effort to avoid repeating the mistakes of the women in her family. By going back to school and working, Janice hopes to improve her family's economic situation and find professional satisfaction. For these reasons, while she identifies with Hope's conflicting feelings about work, unlike Hope she wants to continue working, even when she becomes financially successful. Janice's perceptions about work—anchored in the emotional legacy of her grandmother and her immigrant's hopes for social mobility—thus shaped, and were shaped by, her reading of the television text.

Tamara: "I Feel Really Torn Apart"

For many of the upper-middle-class women I spoke with, there was a sense that *thirtysomething* had in effect been able to portray in stark detail their own often wrenching life decisions. Tamara, a thirty-three-year-old-woman from a well-groomed residential neighborhood in Brooklyn, who was pregnant with her second child at the time of the interview, gave this account:

> What a lot of my friends say is that it sort of seems like they have a microphone in our homes. That they've somehow touched on so many of the values that I have and that people I know share, um, and just in terms of timing. I'm approximately the age of the people on the show, I have a child the age of the lead character's oldest child. I'm having my second child when the lead characters are having their second child. I work part time like the lead character, the wife does. I think politically they are sort of left of center or they purport to be or they were at some point. The way they sort of handle family and work. (transcript no. 8)

In fact, Tamara's life did have some, though by no means all, points in common with the lives of Hope and Michael Steadman. Tamara was Jewish, and married to a Protestant, thereby reversing the husband-Jewish, wife-WASP configuration. Tamara and her husband were both lawyers, though Tamara was working half time at the time of our interview. Tamara came from an upper-middle-class divorced family from Long Island; her mother stayed home full time for a few years, and then went back to work when Tamara was in elementary school. Tamara met her husband, who also came from an upper-middle-class family, while they were in law school and they married soon after. Before she had children, she worked full time at a non-profit environmental agency, but dropped down to half-time work when she had her first child and quit work entirely when her second child was born.

While both Tamara and her husband had made approximately the same amount of money before she cut down to half time, she was currently earning less than a third of what he was earning. (His income was about $60,000 while hers was about $18,000.) Because she and her husband felt that, even with a combined income of $78,000, they could not duplicate the level of middle-class comfort their parents had, they continued to live in a nice middle-class neighborhood in Brooklyn, although with one child and another on the way they wanted to live in a house in the suburbs and not commute tremendous distances.

As Tamara opened the door to her apartment for the interview, I encountered a scene not unlike that of Hope Steadman's world on *thirtysomething*. Tamara was six months pregnant, with a young son leaning against her leg and a cordless telephone propped against her ear. When she got off the phone, she beckoned me into the kitchen, where we talked as she gave her son dinner. Tamara's reactions to *thirtysomething* were organized around the characters of Hope and her struggles over work and family. However, whereas Janice related primarily to

Hope's frustration at being home full time, Tamara identified with Hope's desire to have more time with her young children. Describing her sense of guilt over working while her children were young, Tamara observed:

> Yeah, I think I feel really torn apart. And I feel like ultimately I feel more responsible for my children's development and well-being, but I sort of feel as if I've done that to myself. I know that that's society's expectation. But the way I experience it is as my decision, to feel responsible. I sort of feel guilty when I'm not with my son during the day, because I know other people who are with their children, and part of me feels like nobody can do a better job educating my son and giving him a certain sort of worldview that I have and that I want him to share. But it really seems as if you're able to do that even if you're not with your child full time. But I do feel pulled apart, I feel that I'm not able to be as competent in my career as I want to be, and I feel like, I'm a lawyer, and lawyers tend to work long hours and lawyers that leave work at 5:30 are not taken seriously. It's hard to take myself seriously as a professional. (transcript no. 8)

Although Tamara felt guilty about not being with her child, she also wanted to be taken seriously as a professional. Like Janice, she felt that staying home full time would be unfulfilling. For example, in describing how other mothers in her son's playgroup reacted to the fact that she worked part time, Tamara observed:

> Some of the women who are home full time feel threatened because I am out in the world, I am dealing with adults, I am meeting men, I am given strokes for being competent and adult and in an adult sort of realm. (transcript no. 8)

This sense that women who stayed home full time were threatened by Tamara's participation in the "outside" world is repeated in Tamara's description of Hope Steadman, whom she perceived as frustrated and having low self-esteem because she was not part of the "adult world."

Although she could understand why Hope might be frustrated, Tamara ultimately held her responsible for choosing to stay home. For example, in explaining why she believed the characters on *thirtysomething* were given to "kvetching," or complaining, Tamara talked about how they were part of a generation that tried to challenge traditional social roles but ended up reproducing them:

> I think that they [Hope and Michael] were people who sort of came to consciousness in the sixties and questioned authority and were sort of involved in this upheaval of attitudes and stuff but now they are sort of falling back into fifties style family patterns . . . I think they are sort of people that tried other things and are falling back onto familiar patterns. You know, like, Hope got a college education, from what I can gather. I think they went to University of Pennsylvania, that is like an Ivy League School, so she's very well educated and she did work outside in the world but now she's home with children and resentful that her husband makes gobs of money and she doesn't take herself seriously. I think she has a problem taking herself seriously. (transcript no. 8)

What is perhaps most interesting about Tamara's account of Hope and Michael is that, while she was able to analyze Hope's distress as being rooted in the fact that she came to consciousness in the sixties and is now home full time reproducing fifties-style gender arrangements, she ended up blaming Hope for not taking herself seriously. At the same time, she clearly sympathized with Hope's position. In this sense, Tamara expressed a strong degree of *ambivalence* about the choices available to women, with each option seeming to have its own emotional pitfalls: go to work and deal with feelings of guilt about not becoming a 1950s perfect mom, stay home and deal with loss of self-esteem and self-worth.

In some ways, however, the ambivalence that Tamara felt is probably true of *every* working mother, almost by definition. What makes Tamara unique, however, is her particular identification with the larger historical dilemma that animates *thirtysomething*'s characters: what to do with a worldview that is a core of your identity but out of step with pressing new realities and ego needs? Tamara ultimately resolved her ambiguity through a turn toward individual responses within this social and historical understanding.

In the end, while Tamara could locate Hope's problem as being rooted in larger social circumstances, she ultimately held Hope responsible for her own happiness. Like most people, Tamara bought into the notion that the answer to social problems lies in individual responses. What role does *thirtysomething* play in this process? Tamara often voiced this tension between the "personal" and the "political." Often, this took the form of explaining that, having majored in women's studies in college, she was aware of what it meant for women to live in a patriarchal society. As she would continue speaking, however, she would then get angry at Hope for not taking charge of her life. It was as if through the character of Hope Tamara was working through her own feelings of anger for not being happy in her life. By projecting her anger onto Hope, Tamara seemed to be distancing herself from her own battles with feelings of lack of self-worth. By organizing her thoughts and feelings around an individual character's internal struggles, furthermore, rather than social and historical circumstances, Tamara effectively stopped thinking about the latter. *Thirtysomething* refers to the social, only to appropriate it into the psychological and individual at a deeper level.

So, while Tamara expressed guilt about neglecting her children by working half time, as she began to reflect on Hope's life she became convinced that staying home full time would be equally damaging to her self-esteem. Rather than identify with Hope and sympathize with her decision to stay home full time, Tamara ended up adopting Michael's position toward his wife and chastising Hope for being a bored, unhappy housewife.

Tamara's frustration with motherhood and her idealization of working full time at a creative job came through most poignantly in her attitude toward Melissa, the single character on the show. Melissa was her favorite character and she often spoke as if she would like Melissa's life, as when she observed:

> I sort of envy her freedom and her creativity and her work and her apartment and her younger beau and her just ability to just go and do what she wants and not have to answer to anyone. (transcript no. 8)

At the same time, however, Tamara realized that if she really did have this life, she would feel the social pressure of not having gotten married and had children:

> But I also empathize with [Melissa's] pain in her situation as she measures herself against the Hope and Michael characters and feels like there's something missing, and then I feel, and then when I think of my single friends I feel sorry for them. I think some people are happy to be single and there's a lot of benefits to it and positive things, but I feel badly about a society that says that there is something missing. (transcript no. 8)

Tamara's talk about *thirtysomething* characters thus reflects contradictory feelings about her quite similar life situation. She was wary about adopting a "traditional" domestic role, but was also fearful of what a life might be like without the security of marriage and a family. Perhaps what Tamara's talk most reflects is the tremendous amount of *ambivalence* women experience in trying to negotiate their own expectations of themselves, societal messages of what they should be doing with their lives, and social realities that require them to adopt multiple roles. Most women do not want to give up on the ideal of having a satisfactory work and family life, but beyond the practical obstacles of low-paying work and expensive child care, there simply are not enough models for how this might be achieved. Where those models do exist, they are routinely denigrated in the larger culture as unviable and utopian. Tamara herself pointed this out in her description of *thirtysomething*'s portrayal of its two most non-traditional characters, Gary and Susannah, an idealistic academic and a low-paid non-profit worker who struggle on limited means to enact their commitments to "sixties" ideals, such as sharing work and child care equally:

> It seems like Gary and Susannah are used as a foil that Michael and Hope feel superior to and measure themselves against and they are sort of looked down upon by the writers, I think. They are sort of used as a comedic foil, that I think is unfair because it could really be a beneficial thing to show this very non-traditional family—he was staying home with the baby, and I know people like that, and I think it would be great to have their lives reflected in a positive way, not as a joke and not as something that's being seen as rejecting the family 'cause they're not, they are just different, a new kind of family, and I really hope the world is moving towards accepting new kinds of families. (transcript no. 8)

Despite Tamara's wish that the writers would portray alternative lifestyles in a more positive light, she realized that television's ideology ultimately favors more traditional social arrangements: "I think they [the writers] definitely are geared toward promoting marriage and intelligent women that stay home!" (transcript no. 8) In her own life, Tamara at least temporarily resolved her work/family conflict by choosing to stay home full time after her second son was born. When asked how she felt about her decision, she expressed a great deal of satisfaction and spoke with relish about not having to "wear pantyhose and work under fluorescent lights all day with a bunch of people yelling at each other." Choosing *not* to work thus allowed her to admit the frequently unfulfilling and even oppressive nature of much of work. At the same time, it seemed that she was all too aware of the compromises she had made by staying home and was worried about her ability to re-enter the labor force.

In the meantime, though, Tamara chose to resolve the ambiguities of her life by adopting not Gary's and Susannah's, or even Melissa's, life, but Hope's. Like Hope, Tamara chose for the time being to tend her garden, literally, and when I spoke to her last was watching her garden bear fruit in the suburbs of Maryland, where she eventually moved sometime after the interview. Her youngest child was about to enter pre-school, and she was considering having a third child. Unfortunately, in Tamara's life the vision of shared childcare and work that Gary and Susannah held forth remained as implausible as it was to the writers of *thirtysomething*.

The World of *thirtysomething*: Singling Out Single Women

In many ways, while *thirtysomething* explores what marriage and family means for people who are already "married with children," the program also directs itself to men and women who are not in a permanent monogamous relationship. Many of the most moving and emotionally wrenching episodes deal directly with how depressing it feels to be a *thirtysomething* woman and single. We can see these tensions, first, in interviews I conducted with a group of three middle-class, white single women, Jan, Risa, and Katherine; and second, in the reactions of Irene, a lower-middle-class, divorced mother of two.

Jan, Risa, and Katherine

Jan, Risa, and Katherine were three close friends who had been regular viewers of *thirtysomething* since it began airing. The women, all in their late twenties and living in Park Slope, Brooklyn, seemed to have the style and hipness that *thirtysomething* was trying to emulate. Park Slope is a more urban version of the exurban, mythical Philadelphia-area neighborhood of *thirtysomething*. It mixes urban storefronts with beautiful brownstone rowhouses on tree-lined streets. The residents of Park Slope are predominantly white, non-native New Yorkers, many of whom moved to the neighborhood to raise children. The area is known as a politically liberal yet relatively affluent, family-friendly haven from bustling Manhattan. Shops specializing in children's wear line the main avenue, and strollers clog the sidewalks. Despite this family orientation, the neighborhood includes a growing mix of white, urban singles who have moved to "the Slope" to get more affordable space than was possible in congested Manhattan. Although all three women earned less than Janice and her husband—Jan was earning $15,000 a year as a part-time bookkeeper while she went to school, Risa was earning about $30,000 as a researcher at a public television station, and Katherine was earning approximately $20,000 as a secretary—the neighborhood itself was a far cry from Janice's segregated, crime-infested, crowded, and treeless East New York.

Jan, the first woman who spoke, looked much younger than her twenty-nine years and blended quite naturally with the other undergraduate students at the city college where she was studying. Her determination to persevere—a daunting schedule of work and school—was reflected in the fact that she was training to run in the New York City marathon. Jan began by describing her background. She grew up in a suburb of San Francisco where she was the sixth child in a family of seven. Her father, who was Irish Catholic, worked as a pari-mutuel clerk at a race track while Jan was growing up; his alcoholism had kept him from moving up to a more professional position. Even though Jan's parents owned their own house in a solidly middle-class neighborhood, Jan's father was always trying to juggle the finances to be able to support his large family on a modest income. Nevertheless, Jan never remembers feeling deprived. Jan's own financial circumstances required a juggling act, as she struggled to live in New York while working only part time and going to school full time.

Jan's mother, who came from a German-Catholic family, quit working when she had her first child, despite the fact that she had had in her early twenties a promising career as an administrator for a small company. Jan spoke of her feeling that her mother might have been frustrated having to raise seven children with a husband who was an alcoholic, and wishing that her mother had had the opportunity to develop professionally. While Jan was a young girl, however, her mother was diagnosed with cancer, and she died when Jan was twelve years old. Perhaps because of her mother's early death and her father's alcoholism, Jan felt that her own life had lacked guidance and direction. In her early twenties she lived with a boyfriend in the suburbs, but soon after broke up with him and moved to San Francisco, where she shared an apartment with a roommate and worked in finance at a series of companies. During this period, Jan's life was much more "middle class," as she described it, than it had been in New York. She earned about $30,000 as a junior accountant and had a comfortable apartment with expensive clothes and furnishings.

At the time we spoke, Jan had moved from San Francisco the year before, and was going back to school to finish her B.A. She supported herself through part-time work as a bookkeeper for a small research firm, a job she was dissatisfied with and was looking to change. While at college, Jan became interested in urban planning and was hoping to find a job in this field. She had not seriously dated anyone since her early twenties. Shortly after the first interview, however, she met an architect four years younger than she, and she was struggling to decide whether she wanted to build a future with him.

Risa, Jan's roommate, was also struggling with the idea of being in a committed relationship. Risa was twenty-eight years old, a vivacious and funny Jewish woman with long, dark brown hair, who grew up in a single family house in Midwood, a mixed Jewish and Italian middle-class neighborhood in Brooklyn. Risa had received a B.A. in elementary education from Brooklyn College while in her early twenties. Her father, who was a salesman who owned a series of small businesses, was a very loving man who died while Risa was in her twenties. Risa's mother, who stayed home when she was younger, had been working for a number of years as an office manager for a manufacturing firm in Manhattan. Risa herself had recently made a job change, after working as an elementary school teacher after college. She was now working for a public television station, as a researcher for a children's television program.

Risa had a series of more and less important relationships throughout her twenties. Because she was so attractive and outgoing, she was always meeting men, but she had difficulty finding someone with whom she wanted something more permanent. After the interview, Risa became involved with a man she met at work, but was unsure at the time about the future of their relationship.

Katherine, like Jan, had come to New York from another part of the country in her twenties. Soft-spoken, thoughtful and attractive, she was twenty-nine at the time of the interview. Katherine had grown up in the South and, like Jan, had also come from a large Irish-Catholic family. Her father was a writer who had a number of jobs, and money was also a struggle. Like Risa and Jan, Katherine grew up with a mother who was by and large at home for her chilren, and with a father whose job was never completely secure, despite their middle-class lifestyle. Katherine studied art in college and then came to New York to try to make it as an artist. While still pursuing her artwork on and off at the time we spoke, Katherine was working at the same office as Jan, doing word processing and secretarial work. Like Risa and Jan, after the first interview Katherine got involved in a long-term relationship. Unlike Risa and Jan, however, Katherine moved in with her boyfriend.

All three women were outspoken and reflective about their own lives, describing with more than a little irony their earlier assumptions about where and who they would be at age thirty. Jan first opened up by saying that when she was twenty she had thought that by the time she was "thirtysomething" she would be married with kids and living in a suburb in California, essentially reproducing her mother's life. Risa, who was traveling in Germany when she was twenty, had thought that she would either be married or in a serious relationship, and working as a documentary filmmaker. Katherine was the only one of the three who had not envisioned this scenario when she was twenty, thinking instead she would become a "serious" artist and unsure about her personal relationships.

Of the three, Jan had envisioned the most traditional life for herself, in part because she was in a long-term co-habitational relationship at age twenty. None of the women described their own mothers as particular role models; indeed, their various life courses almost suggest that they had consciously tried to avoid their mothers' fates. Of the three women, only Risa's mother went back to work full time, when Risa was in high school. Both Katherine and Jan cited their older sisters, who had been balancing work and family with greater and lesser success, as more relevant role models.

Describing their fantasies at twenty of who they thought they would be in their thirties proved to be an interesting prelude to Jan, Risa, and Katherine's discussion of *thirtysomething*. For they believed the program was trying to show, in part, how single women were coping with not being in a serious relationship, in a world that expected them, as they had expected themselves, to be "married with children" by the time they hit thirty. They felt that *thirtysomething* was almost a kind of self-exploration of a generation, asking questions like "where are we now" as compared with where we thought we might be. If the question posed for married viewers who grew up with the ideals of the sixties was "how did we end up like our parents?" the question for single women was "how did we *not* end up like our parents?" or more exactly, "just because we did not get married in our twenties, and tried to explore different lives, why do we feel like we've missed the boat when it comes to being able to have a serious relationship?" In fact, both groups of women, single and married, seemed to have conflicting desires about who and what to be at age thirty, and both groups felt a sense of betrayal as if the rules had changed while they were not looking.

When I began to ask these three women about their involvement with *thirtysomething*, and their sense of whether the program was realistic in its portrayal of single, working women like themselves, a whole host of reactions poured forth. Katherine, for example, felt that, although *thirtysomething* was realistic about some issues facing her friends and herself, it fell too much into the trap of trying to put happy endings onto problems that her friends had not been able to resolve in their own lives.

Jan agreed with Katherine that *thirtysomething* was able to raise many of the conflicts she faced, but was not able to leave open the problems in the way she was often forced to in her own life, whether by changing a job she was unhappy with, or leaving a relationship that was not satisfying to her. Describing her frustration with the show's glossing over what had been seemingly intractable problems in her own life, Jan said, "It [*thirtysomething*] brings up things in yourself and you think you can like relate and then when they tie it all up at the end, and in my own life, it's not tied up" (transcript no. 10). When I asked her for an example, she mentioned the ways the couples on the program confront each other and then make up. Risa also mentioned that, even when the couples do not make up in a particular episode, they say really "profound" things she is not able to verbalize in her own life. For these women, the characters' ambivalence and confusion is what makes the show compelling. But the narrative resolutions and the characters' own overarticulateness detract from the realism of the show.

Perhaps not surprisingly, all three women reacted strongly to the portrayal of the single women on the show. First, they all thought that the creators of *thirtysomething* were setting up stereotypes of single versus married women, career versus stay-at-home types, and so on. For example, all three reacted negatively to the portrayal of the career woman character Ellyn Warren. Describing her, Katherine said:

> Ellyn wears sexy underwear and she pushes her body into people's faces and she always has her chest out and she walks like this . . . hardbody. (transcript no. 10)

Jan, too, was annoyed by the portrayal of Ellyn, because she felt that by showing the career woman on the show as a kind of "sex bomb, hardbody, aerobicized person," the writers were setting up a dichotomy between her and the maternal, softer, more humane Hope. Moreover, Jan felt that the program was also setting up a dichotomy *within* Ellyn herself, who was alternately hard-boiled at work and a neurotic, out of control person in her personal life:

> They show Ellyn being flighty even though she's strong in her career, she's kind of always late and bumbling and flighty and about to lose it emotionally. (transcript no. 10)

In fact, when they seriously began to think about the portrayal of Ellyn, the women became increasingly angry. For example, when asked why they had spoken at length about Ellyn, Risa replied that she believed that Ellyn was the most disliked by single women. Katherine agreed, saying that a lot of her own dislike stemmed from the fact that she believed Ellyn's characterization was based on a male perception of what a woman should be like. When I asked them what that perception was, Katherine replied, "Whatever else, if she can get it together in the work world the way a man would, her private life is in shambles" (transcript no. 10). Jan agreed, pointing out that Ellyn's character, more than any other, was constructed around her sexuality: "It's still based on sex, her sexuality" (transcript no. 10).

If Ellyn was the most unappealing character for these women, Melissa was the most interesting. Jan, for example, compared Melissa's ability to be "neurotic" with her own inability to let herself go enough to reveal her own negative, complicated feelings. As Jan observed:

> I always think I would like to be like Melissa because she can be neurotic and I can't be neurotic so I always want to be more like her. I like her alternative lifestyle too. Not Ellyn, because I railed against the corporate thing because I've tried that before. I've tried to work in a corporation and wear a suit and answer to like all these men and it made me sick so . . . I mean looking at Melissa, even though she's this commercial artist, she's doing her own thing. And it's just kind of a dream world, it's like she's got this great loft and you know, and how she makes it from month to month and she might lose this apartment. (transcript no. 10)

Melissa represents the kind of person Jan would like to become, indeed the kind she moved to New York in order to be—a bohemian, expressive, "neurotic" person, whose neurosis, unlike Ellyn's, does not revolve around work habits and sexual tics but around her multiple and complicated emotional connections to others. Jan perceived Melissa to be a lot more human than Ellyn and Hope. She also believed that the way the program portrayed Melissa's relationship with her younger boyfriend was unfair, and seemed to "punish" the character for trying to pursue alternative relationships. Jan was seeing a younger man in her own life, but unlike Melissa, she did not perceive herself as destined to be abandoned because of the age difference. When I asked her specifically what she thought of the episode where Melissa broke up with her younger boyfriend to avoid being abandoned at a later time, Jan opened up:

> It was a very brutal, sad thing. You can't have it all—I mean a young guy is gonna want to go out and experiment around and live life. Melissa is wanting to settle down and have someone to depend on and the timing was all off. All the married couples were having problems having sex and she was having the greatest sex and it was all their relationship was based on, was the sex. There's nothing better than marriage, that's what they were trying to say. It was depressing and bad, I did not like it. But I don't know what the reality of the situation is. I mean in real life . . . I think there are more choices than they show. (transcript no. 10)

Interestingly enough, in this quote Jan seems to be identifying both with the character of Melissa and with the horizon of the show and yet, a moment later, acting as critic.

In general, however, Risa, Jan, and Katherine were frustrated by the narrative resolutions of the female characters, dilemmas that often seemed forced and arbitrary to them. While the situations the characters went through struck a chord, the *resolution* to the situations seemed patently unfair to the single women, and advantaged, they felt, the married women.

The three women also brought up how men were portrayed as points of contrast with the female characters. Katherine, for example, noted that while the men are shown to be conflicted about the choices in their lives, their pain does not seem to wreck their lives and destroy them in the same way it does the women. Jan and Katherine cited the episodes where Elliot had destroyed his life and his marriage by having extramarital affairs. When he was ready to come home, however, he was forgiven and the marriage was stronger than ever. When Michael, too, began to change in the episodes that dealt with becoming more of a "corporate player," they all pointed out that he was basically forgiven for undergoing a radical shift in his identity from "sensitive New Age male" to "hard-boiled career man."

All three felt that, while the men on the show are allowed to have transgressions, the unmarried women are somehow left "out to dry." They cited the character of Susannah as an example of how *thirtysomething* set up single women as immature and out of touch with their "womanhood."

> Risa: Gary's girlfriend was an interesting addition to the show. She was not too sure about this whole motherhood thing but then she totally freaked out about the pregnancy and the pain.
>
> Katherine: But was that surprising? 'Cause she's such a hard person?

Risa: Yeah, she's so negative about everything, and then you hate her.
Jan: They *make* you hate her.
Risa: You just want to tell her to shut up.
Jan: That is also reinforcing this motherhood—marriage thing. Gary and Susannah's relationship just doesn't work. They do not communicate.
Risa: It just makes you also see that kind of woman is not mature, is not as a woman should be, she's out of touch with her emotions, she's out of touch with her mothering, she's out of touch almost with her sexuality, she's out of touch with all the female qualities except for the social worker side. (transcript no. 10)

In this conversation, Risa and Katherine moved from a reading position *inside* the text of *thirtysomething* (e.g., "hating" the Susannah character) to a negotiation of the text as a set of problematic meanings. They assimilate differences between characters to a developmental hierarchy with a strong moral component (e.g., unmarried Susannah is less mature and more out of touch with herself than married Hope) and, moreover, they attribute this hierarchy to an imposition of the makers of *thirtysomething*—the "they" that lies behind the text. But their reading is conditioned, at least in part, by their own perceptions of their social location and their fears and fantasies about its consequences.

In the reading these women viewers have constructed, then, the creators of *thirtysomething* posit women who are unsure about motherhood as basically "screwed up" and men, however confused, unfaithful, and workaholic, as still potentially decent, caring individuals. This sense that the single women (or women who were ambivalent about children) are portrayed negatively on the show was buttressed by their sense that the show makes the "traditional" division of labor between men and women seem the most viable one. For while the married women on *thirtysomething* have their crises, these viewers believed that their lives are ultimately portrayed as the most workable, not only in terms of having enough money to have a good life but also by virtue of the great ideological value the show places on *children.*

Katherine: The traditional relationship is the only one that's working for the kids anyway. It's the one where the mothers are staying home. You know, Nancy and Hope stay home and they are nurturing their kids and they are turning out to be okay. Even when Nancy's little boy was screwed up for awhile, she was still always reaching out and trying to be there for him. And the guys are always there too.

Jan: Even screw-up Elliot came through. . . . I mean the whole thing worked, the relationship, the parenthood worked. Parenthood works. (transcript no. 10)

Even though they all enjoyed the portrayal of the married couples on the program, Risa, Jan, and Katherine found that they related primarily to the single women on the show. This was the case despite their feeling that these portrayals were stereotypical and unfair. When they were asked to describe how they related to the single characters, one key issue that arose was the sense that their lives were not as "settled" as they perceived their married friends' lives to be. This sense of impermanence was due to the fact that they did not have someone with whom they had weathered struggles of various sorts—financial, emotional, sexual—and who had helped them to become less "neurotic." That many married women, especially those in bad marriages, feel completely unsettled did not come up in these conversations. Rather, the consensus was that to be single was to be left prey to a whole series of tangled emotions that could only be resolved with a "home" or stable place to work them through. Katherine was a partial exception. She felt that being married did not necessarily anchor a woman in emotionally volatile waters. In fact, Katherine was more able to identify with what she perceived as the advantage of Melissa's life, in not being *subject to* the vicissitudes of a life partner who might change in unintended and negative ways.

While these single women identified with Melissa, then, and the high-wire nature of her emotional life, they also expressed a great deal of sympathy for Hope. This was the case despite their feeling that Hope was being "set up" by the creators of the program as having the "preferable" life. They all believed that Hope has specific problems that related to being married, that fed into their own anxieties as single women about how marriage might curtail their sense of freedom and self-worth.

For example, both Jan and Katherine mentioned their concern that Hope is often portrayed as struggling with feelings of self-worth because of her conflicts with Michael. Katherine believed this was related to the fact that Hope suppresses the things she wants to do in life in order to keep the family peace. Jan, too, mentioned Hope's possible affair as an example of Hope trying to elevate her self-esteem. Jan believed that Michael does not understand the work involved in Hope's writing an article at home and Hope's frustration that she was not being taken seriously as a professional. Jan felt that Hope finds herself attracted to a man she is working with on the article in part because he, unlike her husband, *does* take her work seriously. That Hope is eight months pregnant at the time only added to Jan's perception that Hope is being desexualized and de-professionalized by her husband.

All three women, in sympathizing with Hope, reacted strongly to what they perceived to be the show's inherent paternalism toward the married female characters. At first, Risa pointed out that she believed the creators of *thirtysomething* perceived themselves as "intelligent men who think they are showing progressive male and female characters" (transcript no. 10). But all three felt that the creators' progressivism masked a condescending view of the married women. Jan noted that *thirtysomething* was progressive for showing Hope and Nancy building these careers from the home, with Hope writing and Nancy making a children's book. But Katherine felt this portrayal was itself a patronizing view of women, because it gave the married women only a limited amount of social power:

> But that's such a condescending view. It's not really necessary that Hope do this or Nancy do that . . . they can have a certain amount of power but not the power to bring home the bacon. Not really the power over the family. You look at those marriages and the power differential, I mean it's not equal. . . . So, I think that's the image they are projecting. It's like women can have a certain amount and it's all peripheral, it's not really integral to making everyday stuff work. Even though they are. Not like a lower middle class woman who has to find someone to take care of her kid and go out and work and even if they are really talented women, go out and be a secretary or something. Everything they do is just as easily something that doesn't have to be done. So the power is all in the men's hands. (transcript no. 10)

Risa continued this line of thought by asking what would happen if the roles were reversed and Michael and Elliot depended on Hope's and Nancy's salaries to survive. She felt that the character Michael would be more interesting as an artist, and she would like to see what it would look like if the couples tried to switch roles as well. This feeling was tied to her sense that the current roles doomed Hope to being stuck in a kind of push-pull with her husband, always trying to be taken seriously.

Thinking about what it would be like if Hope and Michael had more equality in their marriage, Katherine cited Gary and Susannah as one example on *thirtysomething* of a couple who are both struggling to earn a living. Gary's lack of a steady income, however, affects his family in negative ways, as in one episode where they do not have enough money to bring their baby to the emergency room. Citing this episode, Jan observed:

> Yeah, they really played that up, they played up that they were so poor, poor them, they couldn't go out to dinner, they could not afford good medical coverage for their baby, they couldn't afford the doctors that Hope and Michael had. (transcript no. 10)

Katherine also mentioned this episode as an example of how Michael is implicitly held up as being more mature and responsible than his friend Gary for being able not only to support his family but to help Gary out with money when he needs it for family emergencies. Hope is relegated to offering the destitute couple muffins, hardly an expression of great social power.

Ultimately, this sense that Hope is being devalued in the family while Michael is being held up as the paragon of maturity contributed to their anger about *thirtysomething*. Commenting on the double nature of the program, Katherine reflected that, while the show seemed more progressive than other shows on television, it still fed into traditional readings of relations between the sexes. Risa and Jan agreed with Katherine that the program "sucked you in" with its quasi-liberal, "quasi-feminist veneer" (Katherine, transcript no. 10).

When we think about this veneer of feminism more generally in terms of the lives of Jan, Risa, and Katherine, it is interesting to note that all three women were a twentysomething cohort who differed from Tamara precisely in that they had little *direct* experience of or investment in 1970s feminism while it was happening. They did not share Tamara's immediate sense of identification with the worldview of the sixties and early seventies as a core of their self-understanding. They were thus one step removed from personal experience of the women's movement at its most fertile. They got it secondhand: Jan through her recent education, Risa through college, and Katherine through her older sisters. These differences and others had effects on how they understood the feminism of *thirtysomething* and its social claims.

Even within their own age group, Katherine, Risa, and Jan could all be said to have been affected differently by feminism, and the "quasi-feminism" of *thirtysomething* therefore had different meanings for them. Jan, for example, wanted to try to deepen her own life by becoming "more neurotic." Her life thus far was constituted by her emotional blocks and her flight from a chaotic, alcoholic family that also forced her to become economically as well as emotionally self-sufficient at an early age. She expressed the desire to be more able to express herself and "let it out." She saw the articulateness and verbal ability of *thirtysomething* characters—their ability to give voice to what's inside them (one of the show's main conceits)—as a revelation.

Jan is grateful for the quasi-feminism of *thirtysomething*'s female characters: they, at least, know how to represent themselves and their interests in a relationship. They speak up, they talk back and say smart, insightful things:

> They (the female characters) can come out and they verbalize and pinpoint what they are trying to get across. And you can relate to the problems. But in your life you may not be able to identify and concisely wrap it up. (Jan, transcript no. 10)

For Risa, too, the quasi-feminism of *thirtysomething* tapped into struggles she had had in her own life. Risa was exposed to feminism in college as a set of ideas. Contrasted with that was the reality of teaching, a women's profession, which was dehumanizing and oppressive, as was her job at a prestigious children's media firm, where she was stereotyped as "wacky." These experiences may help to explain Risa's cynicism about the world, even feminism itself: no idea can be held as true for very long before it reveals itself as something else. She recognized the small truths that *thirtysomething*'s characters utter (e.g., about the precariousness of single life) but quickly saw how this became part of the show's cynical appropriation of these truths for other ends (selling you images of yourself). Ultimately, Risa saw that what *thirtysomething* offers to a large class of young people like herself is this very cynical posture itself.

For Katherine, finally, the quasi-feminism of *thirtysomething* tapped into still other experiences with feminism. Katherine described having older siblings, one of whom is a feminist artist, who were crucial in giving her a felt sense of feminism as an ongoing struggle to redefine the world, intellectually as well as artistically. This personal connection to the historical period of 1970s feminism was absent for both Jan and Risa. Though her life circumstance were currently similar to Jan's and Risa's, especially her frustrations with financial and emotional instability as a single woman, she experienced *thirtysomething* as having a deeply problematic relation to social reality:

> To me, this is not a progressive show and to me it's just a 1980s version of so many things we saw before. I think we're just really socialized to you know, watch this stuff on tv. It's not exactly real—this has more of a veneer of being real but it's like we're sort of socialized to watch this and not question this is wrong, this is wrong, 'cause it's

> making these tiny advances so you don't want to totally dismiss it. But I think it's very dangerous. That's why I get sort of angry at it, also *Twin Peaks* for those very same reasons. I mean the women, it's just a travesty really, I think. You know, it's not real, but because everyone watches it, it's dangerous. People in a certain demographic group think it's the show to watch and it's sort of cool and you get together and you talk about it. (Katherine, transcript no. 10)

Here Katherine turns her attention from the problem of gender socialization (that *thirtysomething* explicitly thematizes), to the whole problems of media socialization: how we develop a relationship to social reality through media representations. In contrast to Risa's cynicism, Katherine developed an acute skepticism about *thirtysomething*'s representations and more, about informal social discourse about media representations. For Katherine, it was her friends' easy embrace of the "tiny advances" in representing *thirtysomething*'s social reality that was the most dangerous thing of all.

In sum, Risa, Jan, and Katherine had a complex reaction to *thirtysomething*. Like many of the other single women with whom I spoke, these women had mixed feelings about whether the portrayal of the female characters was stereotypical or not. Their recognition that the female characters were often not realistic did not lessen their sense that the program was often accurate in depicting the range of emotions many women feel. The question "Is this realistic?" was a kind of universal framework that arose in almost all the interviews I conducted. It served as a kind of litmus test for the subsequent interest a viewer had in characters, situations, and events on the show.

In terms of specific responses, whereas Katherine had a strongly negative reaction to the portrayal of Hope's life, both Jan and Risa believed that there might be some benefits attached to it, such as a chance to try to communicate better with a man or finally to have a "home." In addition, all three felt that Ellyn's life was portrayed in a negative light, since she was made to be alternatively hyper-sexual and bitchy *and* hard-nosed on the job. Melissa, finally, was perceived as the most sympathetic character. Interestingly enough, of all the characters, the married character Nancy got the most positive reactions from the women, especially after she separated from her husband and became a sexual being again. These women liked the independence that she exhibited during the break-up with her husband, and felt that of all the characters Nancy was the one who had grown the most on the program. Susannah, finally, was a scary character to these women, because they perceived her as being overly cold and incapable of bonding to her child. While they realized this was a kind of stereotype and might even have been a structural means of valorizing more "feminine" characters, they expressed anxiety that they themselves might behave in the same way. As Jan cautioned:

> See, in a realistic sense I would see myself having problems like her with motherhood. I don't have a fear of being overly motherly. It's more like I can't bond to animals, I can't bond to babies. And male-wise it has not been as much bonding as I want! (transcript no. 10)

As the first interview drew to a close, we realized that a new episode of *thirtysomething* was about to be broadcast, and we decided to end the interview by watching it. When the program came on, both Risa and Jan started to laugh at the soundtrack of acoustic guitars, while Katherine rolled her eyes. Once the program began, however, all three women became focused on the dialogue, and throughout the program, all three responded variously to the characters' speech and actions with expressions of disbelief or sympathy.

During the commercials, the women continued to talk at length about what had just transpired, each taking different sides about whether a particular moment was realistic. Although they voiced skepticism at various points, when Melissa entered the bathroom during her art opening and began to cry because a man she had invited had not shown up, the room got very quiet. When the commercial came on, Katherine sat back in her chair, stroking a kitten Risa and Jan had recently gotten. "It's not fair," she finally said, as the third blaring commercial went on the screen. "It's ridiculous that, here Melissa is with her first art opening, and all they can do is show her crying because of a man and running to put on her under-eye cover" (transcript no. 10). While the other women agreed with her that this denigrated Melissa's professional life by showing her as holding up a man's arrival as more important, as soon as the program came back on the air, Jan ran in from the bathroom and Risa quickly sat down and finished pouring the wine. Reaching for the blue organic tortilla chips purchased from the neighborhood food co-op, we all settled in to watch how Melissa resolved being stood up for her date at her first art opening. In this way, *thirtysomething* demonstrated just how successful it could be in drawing female viewers into the "tragic structure" of feeling of "single white females" in late 1980s popular culture. One wonders how much better their talents could have been used had they directed themselves to creating more positive scenarios of strong, independent women forging ahead into uncharted territories.

Irene

While Tamara, Risa, Jan, and Katherine in some respects resemble characters on *thirtysomething*, Irene, like Janice, seems at first to have little in common with these privileged, angst- ridden characters. When I first met Irene, she was thirty-three and working full time as a legal secretary. A regular viewer of *thirtysomething* since its first season, she was divorced and raising two children on her $37,500 a year salary. Her ex-husband contributed about $85 to the household's monthly income. With the exception of the character Nancy, who separates from her husband, Elliot, briefly on the show, Irene's life seemed a far cry from the paired or single world of *thirtysomething*.

Irene was born and raised in Bay Ridge, Brooklyn, a mixed working- and lower-middle-class neighborhood near the Verrazano Bridge, with a population made up of descendants of Italians, Irish, and Scandinavian immigrants. Irene's family was Irish Catholic and her father was a postal worker. Like Jan's father, he suffered from alcoholism. Irene's mother was a housewife, and helped care for Irene's children when they got home from school.

Irene got married at twenty-two, and by the time she was twenty-six she was divorced with two young children, a son and a daughter. Describing herself as a single working mother, Irene was an attractive red-haired woman who dressed in professional suits, with matching costume jewelry necklaces and earrings. At first somewhat shy during the interview, Irene eventually opened up to reveal a wry sense of humor about her own life and spoke movingly of her goals for the future and her hopes for her children.

Irene had worked for most of her adult life and had been doing secretarial work since her mid-twenties. She had been with her legal firm for three years and was frustrated with her current boss, feeling that he condescended to her and accorded her little respect. She had applied for a transfer and was planning on going back to school in the evenings in the fall. While she was unsure about what she wanted to do eventually, she was determined to make changes in her life, and going back for her bachelor's degree, while scary, was something she felt was an important first step. When I asked her whether she was involved with anyone, she said no, and explained how difficult it was to go out and meet people with two children at home.

Irene and I agreed to meet during her lunch hours. Wanting some privacy from her boss, Irene took me into a large conference room, where we began to talk about her watching *thirtysomething*. She said that in the beginning she hated the program because she felt that the characters spent all their time complaining. After reading a positive review, however, she decided to give the show another chance and eventually got "hooked" on it because it dealt with people from her generation:

> I've watched it since the beginning, but I hated it when it first came on. I thought it was a yuppie whining like gross kind of thing just like, Oh my God, everybody's complaining about stuff, about what they did not have. I did not like it. The only reason I went back to it was I think there was a review in the paper that said the first episode was really whiny but the second episode was a lot better. So I thought I'll give it another try. . . . And let's face it, it was the only thing on tv that was dealing with people in my age bracket at that time. It was not *Dallas* or *Dynasty* kind of thing. Without all the glamour. You know people aren't walking around in designer gowns or jewelry and tons and tons of money. They're already settled. They basically deal with real issues . . . It's more general, it's more basic, there are a lot more people who can relate to something that's going on, although I don't know how many people can relate to Michael trying to take over the company!! I mean like your best friend's boyfriend doesn't usually talk about that over dinner, you know what I mean? (transcript no. 1)

What is interesting here is that she explicitly brackets the class dimension as unreal to her, saying, in essence, that that dimension is not important to the larger sense of reality *thirtysomething* has for her. Furthermore, as we noted earlier, for some women class differences seem to account for their feeling that *thirtysomething* characters "complain too much." Like other lower-middle-class women I spoke with, Irene tended to identify not so much with what characters *say* as with the *situations* they are in.

Besides the fact that *thirtysomething* deals with "real" problems that other women of her generation face, Irene also liked it because of its gossip value. She especially loved trashing Hope with her women friends, calling her "Saint Hope" and exclaiming, "I mean, the woman never breaks a dish!" Her friends disagreed with her about Hope, however, and so she enjoyed getting into arguments over characters with them.

When asked why she kept on watching the show through the seasons, even though she felt that the characters were whining yuppies and Hope annoyed her, Irene explained that she felt she could relate to some of the other female characters. Her favorite character, and the one with whom she identified the most, was Nancy:

> Nancy's the only person on the show who has kids who are at this level that basically my kids are at. Ethan's always fighting monsters and stuff like that and she would have problems with Ethan and she would sit there and she would accept him and handle it. I mean, you get the feeling that Hope and Michael would never have Ethan, but Nancy's really cool. She accepts a lot of things and doesn't let that whole moral thing get in the way of how she feels about someone. And that's good and it's bad. You tend to get hurt a lot more. (transcript no. 1)

Clearly, as a divorced mother, Irene identified strongly with the mother figure on the show who was also going through a separation from her husband. Irene perceived Nancy as a "really strong" character, citing her ability to stand on her own and accept people as a qualitiy she would like to have in herself. In this sense, Nancy serves as a model of a mother who can be her own woman, while being there for her children as well. Hope, on the other hand, seems unable to negotiate between being available to others and maintaining her own identity.

While Irene identified with Nancy as a strong, loving maternal figure, she also found herself relating to the character Ellyn, who is portrayed in ways seemingly diametrically opposed to the down-to-earth mother figure Nancy. As a single woman who is scared to make changes in her life and who sometimes does self-destructive things, Ellyn seemed to represent Irene's worst fears about herself. Although Irene's strongest negative reaction to a character was to Ellyn, she spoke at length about her sense that she shared some of the self-destructive qualities that Ellyn demonstrated week after week:

> I don't relate to Ellyn at all, except for the fact that Ellyn is scared all the time. I mean Ellyn is like completely scared about everything. And she just annoys me. She doesn't see, or she refuses to see, what she does to herself. She has no idea who she is, you know, none. She gets what she wants and then she totally screws it up, she runs from it when she has it.

Pausing to reflect on her anger at Ellyn, Irene then continued:

> And that's the thing that I have. I'm kind of looking at myself. So that

> may be why I don't like her. The whole fear of success thing. Like when we were growing up, my father was an alcoholic and my mother was emotionally not there for us. She never supported any of us. It's kind of like you have this feeling you're not really geared toward succeeding at stuff and that's something that I go nuts with my own kids on. It just freaks me out 'cause I don't want them to grow up like that, I don't want them to feel that way. I mean I want them to get their asses kicked a couple of times and I want them to know that's okay. In the big scope of life it doesn't mean anything. (transcript no. 1)

Although Irene felt most positive about the character of Nancy, and felt that Hope, on the contrary, was "just too perfect and too moral and too righteous, like Kennedy kind of almost," when she began to think about the lives of all the women on the program, she immediately cited Hope's life as the most enviable. When asked why she would want the life of a character whom she clearly did not like as a person, she explained that Hope had a life of leisure, with lots of choices available to her. As she fantasized:

> I would like the big house and the backyard and the babysitter to come while I take a bath kind of thing . . . . At this point I want to be married. I want to work three days a week and be married. Not even married, just work part time!! But I would have to be married to work part time. (transcript no. 1)

Here the class dimension reasserts itself: Hope's life seemed enviable because she had the financial resources to work part time, something Irene could not do. Annoyance at Hope's and Michael's complaining can be understood against this same disjunction, one not nearly so compelling for more affluent viewers.

As our conversation progressed, Irene began to describe how difficult life as a single mother was for her, and how marriage was desirable for the financial security it could provide. In addition to financial security, marriage represented to Irene the possibility of coming together again with a man and becoming emotionally and physically intimate, something that had not really happened for her since her divorce four years earlier. In some ways, she felt that she had grown up with false promises that she would be able to find the right man and be able to live "happily ever after." Citing an episode on *thirtysomething* that dealt with video dating, Irene described how difficult it was in reality to find the "perfect man" and how having children made it even harder to get together with a potential partner:

> I think that the eighties have aspired to this whole kind of thing, this position in life kind of thing, you're set up in life with this whole Cinderella thing. You read "Cinderella" to your daughter, it's like, heh, you can work in a grocery store mopping the floor but one day this prince is gonna come along and that's gonna be it and you're gonna go to this big castle, but we all know it doesn't work that way. I mean, it's hard these days, it really is. Like when they went to the dating service, I mean if you're trying to sell yourself what are you gonna say? I pick my nose when I'm home, but hopefully I don't do it in front of you? I don't shower daily? So the show caught a lot of what's going on with the dating problem. It's like if I want to get rid of somebody I tell them I have two kids; if I want to be with somebody I try to keep it out of the conversation. (transcript no. 1)

Faced with the dating problem—having to edit who you are in order to "sell yourself"—Irene saw the dating episode on *thirtysomething* as an apt critique of an impossible situation for women. What she found mirroring her life here was not so much a character as a *situation.* She actively constructed her own account of reality using the narrative situation as merely a scaffolding for her much more dramatic problem, trying to date with children.

The significant aspect of Irene's fantasizing about Hope's life, more generally, is that it provides another example of the class dimension: at a greater class distance from Hope than any other woman except Janice, she was unable to sympathize with her complaints because Hope has so much. The whole problem of "lack of fulfillment in a career" was just not meaningful for her, as it was for the other women viewers. As a struggling single mother from a lower middle-class background, she had no wish to trade places with Hope herself, only with a fantasy in which she could have all the material and emotional comforts Hope has:

> I would love to not be in the city, have some space. I don't need a gigantic house. We're talking about your typical average family type of thing, with some land around it. Do something novel, like plant a garden, that I know nothing about but that would be pretty interesting trying to find out about! And drive the kids to school and then have some kind of obligation to fulfill for a couple of hours while they're in school and then pick them up and just be there. A nice change. (transcript no. 1)

Like Tamara, however, Irene also raised the issue of the drawbacks associated with being home full time, feeling that, at a certain point, women not only become bored but begin to lose their minds. Describing her friend Alice, who was home full time, Irene explained:

> I don't think there's anything wrong with traditional. If you can stay at home and raise your kids, fine. But I think there does come a point where you go mad. My friend Alice, she's got two and she's like totally wacked. And I tell her "get out of the house, Alice, for an hour a week," and she says "I can't." (transcript no. 1)

Unlike Tamara, however, Irene was not making an argument about the need for a fulfilling career; Irene simply recognized that kids are hell to be with, so you need a break.

Many of the other women I spoke with also related stories of friends who were home full time and who were both bored and boring to talk to. Still, the alternative Irene was living was equally frustrating: being stuck in a job with no opportunities for advancement, no relationship, and two children to support was not exactly a recipe for happiness, she concluded. And, in part because of her class background, which did not provide a lot of role models of women with active careers, Irene saw the best alternative as adopting a traditional division of labor with a man and perhaps, if money allowed it, pursuing volunteer work to keep busy. Irene firmly believed that for a woman having a career and caring for one's children were not mutually compatible:

> Let's face it, a career is not your whole life. You can make a career but most people who make a career die old and alone. . . . Let's face it, even with women's lib and all that stuff, it is definitely still a man's world. I wish they were smart enough when they were deciding what role to play in the Dark Ages. They picked the smarter sex to bring up the kids! (transcript no. 1)

As Irene spoke, it became clear that, deep down, she believed that there were real differences between the sexes, especially in their responsibilities to children. She spoke at length about her own ex-husband, and how, even though he had custody three days a week, remained uninvolved in his children's lives. Thinking about her own life, and her relationship with her children, Irene reflected that the bond she had with them was something that could not be matched by their father:

> I think with women and children it's an inner thing, you know, in a lot of ways. Let's face it, you get pregnant, you spend nine months

> with this thing that is not anything, and then all of a sudden you're in charge of somebody's life. It's a scary thing, an awesome thing, not the ninja turtle kind of awesome! I think *thirtysomething*'s saying that it hurts, it hurts, just like when Michael comes home and Hope says, "You haven't even picked her up today." Let's face it, you can lose your job tomorrow and you can work in a sponge factory but when you're home at night, that's still the same. (transcript no. 1)

Irene's reference to losing a job and to factory work makes her class position clearer: she could not and did not assume that meaningful work would be available for her in the way Tamara might; nor did she feel that "mothering" itself conveys intrinsic rewards. She had, rather, a duty and responsibility to her children and also, she was discovering, to herself. Although Irene fantasized, then, about being able to quit work and spend more time with her children, she told me she was not sitting around waiting for Prince Charming to appear at her neighborhood bar. And, despite her feeling that having a career would be difficult to do while raising her children, she was going back to school so she could get a higher-paying job.

Like the character Nancy, Irene was also trying to take charge of her own life after splitting up with her husband and, in so doing, was hoping to provide a good example to her children of attempting things, even if the outcome was unsure. Part of Irene's motivation stemmed from her frustration with a boss who devalued her abilities, as well as an ex-husband who was financially and emotionally unavailable. In this way, she kept returning to Nancy on *thirtysomething*, whom she perceived as also raising herself up after enduring real suffering with a philandering husband and with a bout of ovarian cancer. Describing her anger at Hope at one point, and her feeling that Nancy was more in touch with the difficulties that happen in a less than perfect life, she recounted:

> I think she's [Hope's] really pious, she throws a lot of judgments at everybody. And one of my most favorite scenes was when Nancy turned around and said to her, "You know, one of these days either you're gonna do something or Michael's gonna do something that's gonna rock you to the bottom of your soul and then we'll see what kind of position you're in to talk about anything." (transcript no. 1)

As the interview came to a close, Irene's boss entered the conference room and asked Irene where a revised version of a document was that he had given her before she went to lunch. "It's on my desk," she replied calmly, with a hint of anger at having him interrupt her during our session. Not acknowledging his secretary's annoyance, he continued, "When are you coming back? We need to get the affidavit out by 2:30." She responded, this time more clearly exasperated, "I'll be there in five minutes!! Just take it easy. Maria's there if it's an emergency." Never losing his composure, her boss joked, "But you know there's no one who can do it as well as you!" and hurried out of the room in search of Maria. I asked Irene if this was a typical interaction between the two of them, with her boss putting subtle pressure on her and her giving him "backtalk" but acceding to his wishes. She nodded yes.

This brief window on Irene's work life provides an interesting epilogue for thinking about Irene's class situation: as a worker who is a secretary, she has become adept at micro-managing a relationship in which she has little if any real power. The fact of her lack of social and economic power is crucial for her reading of *thirtysomething*. In this sense, Irene's identification with Nancy may reflect her sense that Nancy, because of her separation from her husband, has a similar lack of economic and social power. Nancy's own strategies of micro-management within a restricted area—respecting her children, trying to take herself seriously— are what capture Irene's imagination. From this vantage point, Hope's life and worries are indeed remote and suitable for nothing more than idle fantasy.

Conclusion

For each of the women I interviewed, *thirtysomething* was a vehicle for identifying with female characters and describing their own conflicts over love, work, and family. Most found that the show succeeded in raising issues they too were struggling with. Where it seemed to ring less true for these women was in the *resolutions* made available to the female characters. Only the most privileged women I spoke with felt that the various options that a character like Hope could choose might also be realistic possibilities for them. More often than not, the female viewers had to content themselves with relating to the situations that the female characters confronted, rather than the choices they made. Still, the positive associations that women like Irene had with certain characters, such as Nancy for her courage, or Melissa for her openness and vulnerability, did give the women some vehicle for imagining their lives in different ways. In this sense, *thirtysomething* served as a projection screen for women, spurring them to think about new scenarios in their own lives. Almost inevitably, however, the changes they wanted to effect in their own lives required making larger changes in the society, such as increasing women's (and men's) wages and job security, making affordable daycare available, and creating male partners capable of and interested in sharing domestic responsibilities equally. These changes were happening extremely slowly, which left many of the women I spoke with angry, confused, and hostile at themselves and their limited options.

Thus, while *thirtysomething* had a place in these and other women's lives in helping them to think through gender conflicts, its use value was constrained by larger social contexts that made personal changes difficult, if not impossible, to achieve. Moreover, its use was also constrained by the text itself, in its narrative and formal strategies for constructing "plots"—and often burying multiple contradictory meanings about gender in them. *Thirtysomething*, for example, often failed to connect individual female characters' conflicts to the larger social and historical terrains, instead portraying problems as individual in nature and requiring individual solutions. It did this despite making the personal and shared histories of its characters a central theme. In these ways, *thirtysomething* continually opened up a dialogue with the viewers, and then closed off the ways different issues could be thought about, as it followed the larger culture's prescriptions for women.

In conclusion, *thirtysomething* was successful in opening up a terrain for reflection-on history, on gender conflicts—for its female viewing audience. At the same time it foreclosed certain meanings and preferred others. The women I spoke with nevertheless used *thirtysomething* in ways that we, as critics and academics, may not expect. For example, women's readings are often different, and reflect their personal lived histories as subjects. Nevertheless, their lived histories, and hence their readings, reflect their social locations (both class and to some extent, race and marital status and age), and these partly shape and constrain the ways they read, and the meanings they make, about the program. In this sense they are, as Ien Ang articulated it, active but not *powerful.* For the most part, they cannot think through the contradictions and lack a meaningful vocabulary (in Robert Bellah's sense) for imagining alternative scenarios.

Notes

1. These domestic shows, as Patricia Mellencamp has pointed out, in reality contained family conflicts through the medium of humor, with the situation comedy becoming a primary genre for depicting family life in the 1950s (Mellencamp 1986).

Chapter Six

Conclusion: Life After *thirtysomething*

In a 1989 poll conducted by Time/CNN, women were asked to select the most important goal for the women's movement today. The participants rated "helping women balance work and family" as the number one goal, and as the second goal "getting government funding for programs such as child care and maternity leave" (Wallis 1989). Other studies conducted by news organizations pointed to women's frustration with balancing the demands of work and family (Belkin 1989; Cowan 1989). These polls and studies reflect the fact that while women have entered the labor force in historically unprecedented numbers, this new historical reality has not resulted in corresponding changes in either the division of labor between the sexes or the adoption by government of changes in childcare and maternity leave policies. As a result, middle-class women experience both external stress and internal turmoil, often doing "second shifts" of domestic and emotional work, juggling childcare and job, and doubting their adequacy at both.

In trying to explain why most women seem to put up with this situation, reporters and researchers offer a variety of theories. Some believe that women put up with an unfair load at home because of the wage gap between men and women—that women feel they have to put in more work at home in order to make up for earning less. Arlie Hochschild has pointed out, however, that in homes where women earn more than their husbands, women nevertheless continue to do most of the home labor, and she theorized that it may be in part to protect the male's ego from the female's higher wage (cited in Cowan 1989). A third, more plausible theory is that women in fact resent this double burden but suppress their resentment in order to keep the marriage from falling apart.

Thirtysomething, I have argued, drew on these contemporary frustrations and anxieties as central to its strategy for reaching its affluent target audience. Todd Gitlin, commenting on this capacity of network television to hone in on prevailing flash points in American culture, notes:

> Sometimes network television seemed to succeed in packaging images that drew on unresolved tensions in the society. Cramming these tensions into the domesticated frame of the sitcom and the action-adventure, television, whether "realist" or "escapist," clearly bore some relation to the real world, even if only the real world of popular desire and fear . . . these shows demonstrated that television could be popular not by ducking reality but by doing something else to it; not reproducing it exactly, but squeezing some version of some truth into the conventions of an already established form. (Gitlin 1985:12)

Within this framework, *thirtysomething* may be viewed as a particularly successful attempt to package the anxieties that women feel over trying to manage the increasing burdens of work and family and maintaining relationships with men and women.

In trying to reach its target audience, then, *thirtysomething* drew on the frustrations that women felt over work and family. In this process, it itself became one cultural site where questions about women's changing social roles were posed in a public format. As Paul Hirsch and Horace Newcomb point out, television is a key arena where social questions are continually raised. Programs like *thirtysomething* may be most interesting for revealing the way in that questions are allowed to be posed, more than any given answer they offer to a specific problem:

> We suggest that in popular culture generally, in television specifically, the raising of questions is as important as the answering of them . . . Put another way, we argue that television does not present firm ideological conclusions—despite its formal conclusions—so much as it comments on ideological problems. (Newcomb and Hirsch 1984:63)

Thirtysomething's comments on the ideological problem of gender include presenting thematic narratives that address and then resolve women's gender conflicts in traditional ways, as well as creating specific social types of female characters who are either "losers" or "winners" according to the degree to which they approximate the marriage/motherhood ideal. In this way, *thirtysomething* worked to privilege traditional gender roles, even as the society at large could no longer support a strict adoption of these roles. When reading *thirtysomething* symptomatically, one is then led to ask why traditional gender roles were being valorized at precisely the historical moment when they could no longer be supported by changing social conditions.

Assumptions about traditional gender roles have been in force for such a long time, and carry such a large emotional weight, that it is probably unrealistic to expect that they would simply disappear in the first wave of historical change. Traditional gender roles exert such a tremendous force in constituting our very identities that it makes sense that a cultural product would still hold those as a cornerstone in constructing their narratives. This slowness with respect to changing assumptions about traditional gender roles is based on a larger political axiom that asserts that changes in consciousness follow from changes in social conditions. However, the speed at which changes in consciousness occur may lag far behind the actual changes that have occurred in society. So, even though the world has changed, ideas about the world may still accord with how the world "used to be." Although most women are in fact leading very different lives from those of their mothers, expectations about their roles and, more generally, about what is appropriate and inappropriate for a woman to do may be closer to the expectations for their mothers than for their daughters.

A second possible reason why *thirtysomething* offered traditional gender roles in a period of historical change, in line with Newcomb's and Hirsch's reading of television as serving as the site for the airing of social conflicts, is that it offered individuals a means by which to resolve the anxieties engendered by recent social changes. Here the concept of nostalgia plays a key role. Nostalgia for earlier times is evoked as a constant theme on the show whenever a character finds a situation in the present to be anxiety-producing. Unlike straightforward nostalgic shows constructed to evoke memories of supposedly happier earlier eras (such as *The Waltons*), nostalgia on *thirtysomething* is often offered with a wink and a nod, that is, with the understanding that the viewers know the characters, and they themselves, are "playing" with the earlier social roles rather than re-creating them un-self-consciously. What this does is draw the viewers into the structure of feeling for nostalgia even more deeply by reassuring them that they are keeping an ironic distance. For the supposedly knowing subjects of an anxiety-filled present, ironic nostalgia offers a means of resolving these anxieties in perhaps more effective ways than even more straightforward nostalgic texts such as *The Waltons*, that are historically delineated as being in fact in the past.

A third reading of the regressive messages on *thirtysomething* must be seen within the context of feminism itself. The women's movement of the 1960s and 1970s fought long and hard to make changes in women's lives that might allow women to integrate their work and family lives meaningfully in the same way that men had recently been afforded, including federally funded daycare, pay equity, and flexible work hours. These cornerstones of the women's movement have not been realized at the national level, despite feminists' efforts. Society has been extremely slow to accommodate itself to women's changing roles and has instead let women bear the primary burdens for the social and economic changes that necessitated their entry into the paid workforce. Men, for the most part, have failed to fight for these changes, and have done little on the homefront to equalize the burdens of domestic work.

Given these realities, many women are experiencing a high degree of dissatisfaction with their lives. Unlike men, who are encouraged to pursue their careers and who have also been recently encouraged to be more engaged in their family roles, women are made to feel that they are short-changing one or the other sphere and are therefore unsuccessful in both areas. In this sense, resistance to feminism in the larger culture has been extremely effective, precisely because feminism has now become a scapegoat for women's frustration, since it was supposedly responsible for giving them too high expectations of what they could achieve. That the men in their lives are still allowed to and are now encouraged to become "new fathers" at the same time they pursue careers is never questioned. Popular texts like *thirtysomething* carry an implicit rebuke to the women's movement for holding out such "impossible" goals for women of "having it all."

Thirtysomething may thus be read symptomatically, as part of a cultural and ideological process of scaling back women's expectations for themselves and their lives. It is possible to view the show as an arbiter signaling a period of re-adjustment and normalization of scaled-back goals for women, their images of what is and what is not possible to achieve in their lives. It is in this sense that Gitlin's and Hirsch's and Newcomb's formulations that television shows "comment" on prevailing social and ideological problems seem most apt.

Looking at artifacts such as *thirtysomething* can help us understand how popular cultural narratives help lay the groundwork for women's resignation and accommodation to an increasingly intolerable situation. For such narratives function, I have argued, as a means of making women feel guilty and resentful, both about departing too far from traditional roles and about embracing those roles. This in turn lessens their ability to react to their life situations with feelings other than guilt and resentment. Once these narratives have constructed a woman's gender crises in these terms, the solution is ultimately re-inscribed in the domain of her subjectivity, rather than in the social order. Popular narratives that view women working outside the home as the problem implicitly invite their viewers also to feel guilty about assuming this new role. After laying the guilt on the doorstep of the woman, they invite her to expiate her guilt through compromises, therapy or resigned acceptance of her fate. Betty Friedan, in her second manifesto to women, *The Second Stage*, comments on the guilt that is produced by the demands placed on women. She likens this guilt to the guilt women experienced in pre-feminist days that had prompted her to write *The Feminine Mystique.* Describing the sources of this new guilt, she writes:

> The guilts of less-than-perfect motherhood and less-than-perfect professional career performance are real because it's not possible to "have it all" when jobs are still structured for men whose wives take care of the details of life, and homes are still structured for women whose only responsibility is running their families. (Friedan 1986:355)

Thinking about contemporary sources of guilt for women, we can look not only to programs like *thirtysomething* but to other narratives targeted toward women during the same period. Some mass cultural narratives of the 1980s, for example, did not always set up such a strict distinction between work and family as *thirtysomething*, but rather exhibited a plethora of different messages or meanings surrounding women's re-entry into the labor force. Some narratives idealized the working woman as indeed a "superwoman," able to have it all. Later in this period, however, one finds a kind of "backlash," where the idea of "having it all" is seriously questioned. At both points, however, the entire phenomenon of women entering the labor force is greeted as conflicting with traditional gender identities, whether for good or ill, and thus always as constituting some kind of problem to be mediated.[1]

Another way we can begin to characterize the kinds of discourses about working woman of this time is to compare them to the years in that the baby boomers' mothers were raising children, 1950-1959. While the prefixes "pre" and "post" present terminological difficulties in the sense of artificially assigning a precise periodization to historical eras that were not characterized by radical breaks so much as gradual transformations, I think it is useful to describe the historical period of 1950-1959 as "pre-feminist," in that it marks the time prior to watershed events in the struggle for women's rights, including the publication of Betty Friedan's *The Feminine Mystique* (1963), the proposal of the Equal

Rights Amendment (1967), the Strike for Equality Day in New York City (1970), and the debut of *Ms. Magazine* (1972) (Wallis 1989).[2]

Many of the cultural narratives produced in this period cautioned women against working outside the home. Numerous commentators on popular films of this era, for example, have pointed out that the messages of these films was that women who work outside the home experience a loss of their femininity and a crisis in their traditional gender identity (Haskell 1987; M. Rosen 1973). This gender crisis can be seen in any number of films of that period, from *Lucy Gallant* with Charlton Heston and Jane Wyman to Douglas Sirk's *Imitation of Life* (1959), where the woman is always portrayed as having to choose between her desire for a career (to be an actress or shop owner in these two films) and her desire to marry the man she loves, who, of course, refuses to let her work. The dilemma evoked in these cultural texts was conceptualized as the impossibility of being a full time wife and working woman, and the selfishness and false pride of the women who wanted to have a career outside the home.

Present-day narratives about women who work represent in some respects a departure from the pre-feminist cultural discourses of the 1950s, while in others a re-affirmation of the most conservative messages of that earlier period. On the one hand, some narratives portrayed women as being able to have it all, to be superwomen, and so on. On the other, one finds a number of morality tales in this era about women who work outside the home: that they will have difficulty finding and keeping men; that their biological clock will tick away and thwart them from having a family; that they will be lonely, depressed and anxious if they pursue their career singlemindedly unless they find a man to teach them how to "relax" and not take themselves so seriously; that, finally, the decision to remain at home with their children is ultimately a more mature decision in some ways than the need to prove something by going out to work. Real happiness is construed in many of these narratives as lying, not in one's work, but in the cultivation and development of one's family life. That society itself is structured in such a way that women are forced to choose between a full-time job and a family life is never questioned. Rather, the narratives always posit the phenomenon of working outside the home as itself the cause of various dilemmas.

Thus, despite the fact that the popular films and television shows of the pre-feminist 1950s and the post-feminist 1980s are separated by time and, more important, by the revolution in women's lives in the past twenty years, there is nevertheless a similar narrative structuration that women working is a *problem* that requires various personal solutions. It is thus instructive to compare the narratives of the 1950s and 1980s, for all their differences, in order to understand the pervasiveness, despite the gains in women's equality, of traditional gender identities that consider women working outside the home to constitute a "crisis" vis-à-vis traditional femininity.

This, then, is the ideological "conclusion" or closure of *thirtysomething* as a text. But as Hirsh and Newcomb point out, texts do not close down meaning so much as open it up. In particular, this closure is in tension with a countervailing tendency of *thirtysomething* to put the "crisis" and the attending feelings of guilt and resentment *in* the characters' lives and in their mouths. It thus invites viewers to think about these problems in their own lives. This is the "liberatory" moment in *thirtysomething.*

Perhaps the most unique aspect of *thirtysomething* was that it tried, unlike most American television, to have its characters speak self-consciously about their historical and class status as young, urban professionals who grew up in the 1960s. Rather than take for granted their relatively privileged status, each week the characters of *thirtysomething* agonize over a particular issue that confronts them as a result of having too many, rather than too few, choices in life.

This self-consciousness about their privileged lives may alienate many viewers, particularly those from less than middle-class backgrounds, who resent the fact that every week this group of "yuppies" come on television, and complain endlessly about their clearly affluent lifestyle. And yet, as Sut Jhally and Justin Lewis have pointed out, the same viewers who dislike these "whining yuppies" so intensely can nevertheless enjoy watching the upper-middle-class lives of the Huxtables on *The Cosby Show,* who un-self-consciously live out their class status as black professionals and invite all America, rich and poor, to identify with their weekly family exploits (Jhally and Lewis 1992:134). In so doing, they act like "normal" families on television, who are precisely upper middle class but do not dwell at length on their privileged status. Many viewers' initially negative reaction to the agonizing on *thirtysomething* may not be simple class resentment, then, but a mixture of other things, including a general resistance to thinking about class and an unfamiliarity with the style of discourse of *thirtysomething*'s characters, that is highly subjective, ironic, and self-revealing.

Interestingly, for the women I interviewed, initially negative responses waned over time as they sought a meeting ground with the world of *thirtysomething*'s characters. Lower-middle-class women became as faithful viewers of the show as upper-middle-class women. I have suggested that *thirtysomething*'s portrayal of gender-role conflicts, in particular women's struggle to reconcile the competing demands of work and family, became a key meeting ground for viewers from otherwise different backgrounds. "Gender," in this sense, became a way of overcoming and incorporating the problematic of "class." For the women who became regular viewers of the program, from both the lower and upper middle classes, what drew them in each week were *situations* in that female characters found themselves struggling with changing gender roles. For upper-middle-class women, furthermore, there was the sense that the language the characters used to describe their conflicts articulated their own sense of anxiety. Lower-middle-class women, while put off by the "complaining" of the female characters—that is, by their need to constantly verbalize their discontent—nevertheless also identified with the situations in which the female characters found themselves. Thus, even when some of the lower middle-class women voiced their antipathy toward the privileged lives of the characters, they were willing to suspend their frustration at watching yuppies self-consciously complain about their lives when the situations which the fictional yuppie women were confronting were portrayed.

Gender and the Construction of Meaning

Thirtysomething's exploration of women's gender role conflicts offers an important cultural site from which to view these ideas and social myths concerning women's ambivalent feelings about their changing social roles. Female viewers constructed meanings about their own lives, furthermore, by interpreting these social myths. Women identified with the struggles that the female characters of *thirtysomething* had over issues of gender. They repeatedly described how they had "felt like" a particular female character at one point in their lives, and that they could "relate" to a specific female character and the problems she was having. This process of identification often took the form of describing how they could see a "little bit of themselves" in each female character, rather than finding a one-on-one identification with any individual character.

This finding that female viewers identify with the female characters and the situations they find themselves in confirms other studies of female viewership, particularly those undertaken by Press, Radway, Ang, Bobo, and others. Andrea Press' work on class differences and women's identification with television characters, for example, explores how female viewers, both working class and middle class, constructed identifications with the situations that privileged female characters found themselves in. Writing about working-class women, for example, Press notes that

> Working-class women consistently and repeatedly define shows to be "realistic" when they depict lifestyles that are much more affluent than that of their own, or even than that of the average middle-class American. Many go so far as to compare events and problems of their own lives to those depicted in middle-class shows, even when the scale of money involved in these two sets of events differs radically. (Press 1987: 212)

Press attributes this identification to what she calls a "hegemony of middle-class realism" that exists for working-class women, who come to experience as normal the vast majority of images of middle- and upper-middle-class women on television. Jacqueline Bobo, in addition, through her research on African-American viewers of the film *The Color Purple,* tries to understand how these women form positive identifications with the female characters in the film. As she notes:

> Black women have demonstrated that they found something useful and positive in the film. Barbara Christian relates that the most frequent statement from Black women has been: "finally, somebody says something about us." This sense of identification with what was in the film would provide an impetus for Black women to form an engagement with the film. (Bobo 1988:101)

Bobo utilizes the encoding/decoding model first introduced by Stuart Hall, Tony Bennett, David Morley, and others at the Birmingham Centre for Cultural Studies in order to understand how women can construct positive identifications from mass cultural texts (Bobo 1988:96). These theorists in the cultural studies tradition look at the ways in spectators' cultural backgrounds play a role in their interpretation of a text. Since a program can never firmly guarantee that a specific meaning will be derived from it, the question of meaning must ultimately be considered an open one. As David Morley has observed:

> The text, of course, may offer the subject specific positions of intelligibility, it may operate to prefer certain readings above others; what it cannot do is to guarantee them-that must always be an empirical question. This is, in part, because the subject that the text encounters is, as Pecheux has argued, never a "raw" or "unacculturated" subject.

> Readers are always already formed, shaped as subjects, by the ideological discourses that have operated on them prior to their encounter with the text in question. (Morley 1989:21)

The research undertaken by Bobo and Press is similar in that both focus on viewers' responses as well as on the cultural texts themselves. Both Bobo and Press find that viewers interpret these texts in terms of their own lives. Viewers use fantasy and imaginative projection not simply to "escape" reality but to come to terms with that reality. These scholars explicitly take into account the ways an individual's cultural background may influence this process: for Press, the key social dimension is class; for Bobo, it is race.

This study focuses, with some exceptions, on white, urban, middle-class women. My goal, like Bobo's, is to see how a specific social group reacts to representations targeted to that group. But I examine two clusters of women within the broad, ill-defined category of "middle class"—lower- and upper-middle-class women—because, like Press, I am interested in how class becomes articulated in relation to popular culture. What unites this work to the research undertaken by these feminist scholars is the shared belief that women do in fact read popular culture in terms of their own social locations and experiences and that these experiences shape and constrain, in return, the meanings that can be made. Popular culture becomes a site that women can draw on to construct accounts of their own lives, but these accounts vary according to the ideological discourses that have shaped particular readers as subjects.

Taking seriously this understanding of popular culture's importance for constructing meanings about our lives, Ien Ang has described the ways popular culture produces a series of fictions, which she defines as "collective and public fantasies; they are textual elaborations, in narrative form, of fantastic scenarios" (Ang 1990:84). Among these fictions are female characters who, according to Ang, do not themselves consist of unitary "subject" positions and thus do not offer one firm identity, but rather are a "site" of a "multiplicity of subject positions." This multiplicity within any female character, in turn, is also evident in female viewers themselves, who may occupy a series of different "subject" positions or, as I refer to them throughout this study, social roles, in real life (Ang 1985:85).

Ang goes on to observe that the women's movement has in a sense intensified for women this problem of which "subject" position they should be adopting, because women are now more conscious of their position in society and of their ability to adopt new roles. All of this suggests that to be a woman today involves more work than ever, that is, each woman must in a sense try to invent herself within the maelstrom of cultural messages and social roles now available to her. She cannot count on being able to fall back on a well-worn path of femininity, but must choose what kind of woman she will be at each point in her life:

> Being a woman, in other words, can now mean the adoption of many different identities, composed of a whole range of subject positions not predetermined by immovable definitions of femininity. (Ang 1985:85)

Ang concludes that the public fictions offered by television programs such as *Dallas* and, I would argue, *thirtysomething* can play a role in this process of self-construction by women, in that they offer a series of different subject positions or modes of femininity that the individual female spectator symbolically adopts or reacts to in thinking about her own life (Ang 1990:83).

Like Ang's female viewers of *Dallas*, many of the women I spoke with tended to project onto *thirtysomething*'s female characters their own attitudes about what they thought was the best course of action a woman could take, what behaviors they considered appropriate, what conflicts they saw as arising for women. Although these projections may be fantasies, then, in the sense that each female viewer is not "really" like the female character whose position she is symbolically adopting, the work of imaginative projection nevertheless fulfills an important function for viewers, by allowing them to explore the different social roles they are called upon to occupy and their ambivalent feelings about these roles.

Of course, I have argued, to the extent that programs like *thirtysomething* frame how women can understand their social roles and to the degree that these "frames" are inherently conservative, women's freedom to imagine their lives is indeed constrained by the terms of the narratives. Thus, the positive potential of shows like *thirtysomething* to address women's lives must ultimately be measured against the ways the show "positions" women to interpret their own lives with resignation. A feminist practice for the 1990s must therefore be able simultaneously to address women's sense of conflict over their roles, which *thirtysomething* was so effectively able to do for a significant group of women, and to counteract cultural messages that admonish women to "pack it up" and go home. It must also challenge the nostalgic subjective and individualistic readings of social, economic, and political problems that popular culture perpetuates. In particular, it must include an analysis and critique of the ways that commercial media—whether prime-time drama, advertising, or popular novels—tend to sell women's interior lives back to them in exchange for domestic and political quiescence. Rather than construct feminism as a set of foreordained consumer "choices" between one realm or the other (home or work), a feminist practice must focus on challenging the Machiavellian choices women are now often forced to make. It is not that women simply need the freedom to choose; rather it is that the language of "choice" itself reflects a narrow consumer ethic or culture.

We should encourage freedom to choose motherhood for those women who want to be mothers and freedom to choose otherwise for those who do not. Being a loving mother should not and cannot be mutually incompatible with being an active member of the paid workforce. It is not unreasonable to desire fulfillment in both love and work, and it is a human right to pursue both with all the human energy and creativity at one's disposal. If we are all capable, as Sara Ruddick has pointed out, of thinking "maternally," then we should all be capable of pursuing a satisfying work life as well.

Many changes in current social arrangements are necessary before these visions can be fulfilled for all women. Advances in career access and pay equity, workplace flexibility, family and childcare policy, and men's willingness and ability to share equally in domestic labor are all crucial. Changes will occur for middle- and upper-middle-class women before they do for poorer women. Already, immigrant and working-class women of color are bearing an unequal share of the hardships of current arrangements, since, as low-paid caregivers and housekeepers for more affluent working women, they often struggle with great difficulty to meet their own families' needs.

A feminism re-committed to theorizing not just women's objective oppression but the subjective conditions of its overcoming for all classes and colors of women is necessary to achieving these transformations. Such a feminism will need to look into, through, and ultimately beyond pop cultural texts and discourses, the house of mirrors in which contemporary women continually find and lose themselves.

Notes

1. There have been many interesting explorations into the rise of the so-called "therapeutic culture" in the United States in this century, and I think, in terms of my own research into the kinds of solutions offered to women to resolve their gender crises, these studies will be useful. Among the treatments that seem most helpful are Reiff (1966) and Lasch (1978).

Bibliography

Adorno, Theodor. (1975) "Culture Industry Reconsidered." *New German Critique* 6: 12–19.

Adorno, Theodor and Max Horkheimer. (1972) "The Culture Industry: Enlightenment as Mass Deception." In Horkheimer and Adorno, *Dialectic of Enlightenment,* trans. John Cumming. New York: Continuum.

Allen, Jeanne. (1980) "The Film Viewer as Consumer." *Quarterly Review of Film Studies* 5 (Fall): 481–499.

——. (1988) "Looking Through *Rear Window*: Hitchcock's Traps and Lures of Heterosexual Romance." In *Female Spectators: Looking at Film and Television,* ed. E. Deidre Pribram. New York: Verso.

Allen, Robert C. (1985) *Speaking of Soap Operas.* Chapel Hill: University of North Carolina Press.

——, ed. (1987) *Channels of Discourse: Television and Contemporary Criticism.* Chapel Hill: University of North Carolina Press.

Anderson, Margaret L. (1988) "Feminism and Social Reform: Liberal Perspectives." In Anderson, *Thinking About Women: Sociological Perspectives on Sex and Gender.* New York: Macmillan.

Ang, Ien. (1985) *Watching Dallas: Soap Opera and the Melodramatic Imagination.* London: Methuen.

——. (1989) "Feminist Desire and Female Pleasure." *Camera Obscura* 17:179–191.

——. (1990) "Melodramatic Identifications: Television Fiction and Women's Fantasy." In *Television and Women's Culture: The Politics of the Popular,* ed. Mary Ellen Brown. London: Sage.

Auletta, Ken. (1991) "The Network Takeovers: Why ABC Survived Best." *New York Times,* Sunday, July 28, p. 20.

——. (1992) *Three Blind Mice: How the TV Networks Lost Their Way.* New York: Vintage Books.

Baca Zinn, Maxine and D. Stanley Eitzen. (1990) *Diversity in Families.* New York: Harper and Row.

Baehr, Helen. (1980) "The 'Liberated Women' in Television Drama." *Women's Studies International Quarterly* 3: 29–39.

Bathrick, Serafina. (1984) "The Mary Tyler Moore Show: Women at Home and at Work." In *MTM: "Quality Television,"* ed. Jane Feuer et al. London: British Film Institute.

Barrett, Michele. (1980) *Women's Oppression Today: Problems in Marxist Feminist Analysis.* London: Verso.

Barthel, Diane L. (1988) *Putting On Appearances: Gender and Advertising.* Philadelphia: Temple University Press.

Barthes, Roland. (1972) *Mythologies.* New York: Hill and Wang.

——. (1975) *S/Z.* London: Cape.

Baudrillard, Jean. (1983) *Simulations.* New York: Semiotexte.
Belkin, Lisa. (1989) "Bars to Equality of Sexes Seen as Eroding, Slowly." *New York Times,* Sunday, Aug. 20, Section 1, pp. 1, 26.
Belsey, Catherine. (1980) *Critical Practice.* London: Methuen.
Benjamin, Jessica. (1988) *The Bonds of Love: Psychoanalysis, Feminism, and the Problem of Domination.* New York: Pantheon.
Bennett, Tony. (1982a) "Text and Social Process: The Case of James Bond" *Screen Education* 41: 3–14.
——. (1982b) "Theories of the Media, Theories of Society" In *Culture, Society and the Media,* ed. Michael Gurevitch et al. New York: Methuen.
Bennett, Tony and Janet Woolacott. (1987) *Bond and Beyond: The Political Career of a Popular Hero.* New York: Methuen.
Bennett, Tony et al., eds. (1981) *Popular Television and Film: A Reader.* London: British Film Institute/Open University Press.
Berman, Marshall. (1988) *All That Is Solid Melts into Air: The Experience of Modernity.* Harmondsworth: Penguin.
Bernard, Jesse. (1989) "The Good-Provider Role: Its Rise and Fall." In *Family in Transition: Rethinking Marriage, Sexuality, Child Rearing, and Family Organization,* ed. Arlene S. Skolnick and Jerome H. Skolnick. Glenview, IL: Scott, Foresman.
Blau, Eleanor. (1990) "Can "thirtysomething" Fans Accept a Bout with Cancer?" *New York Times,* Jan. 22, p. C14.
Bobo, Jacqueline. (1988) "The Color Purple: Black Women as Cultural Readers." In *Female Spectators: Looking at Film and Television,* ed. E. Deidre Pribram. New York: Verso.
Boddy, William. (1983) "Loving a Nineteen-Inch Motorola: American Writing on Television." In *Regarding Television: Critical Approaches—An Anthology,* ed. E. Ann Kaplan. American Film Institute Monograph Series, vol. 2. Frederick, MD: University Publications of America.
Bottomore, Tom et al., eds. (1983) *A Dictionary of Marxist Thought.* Cambridge, MA: Harvard University Press.
Bourdieu, Pierre. (1980) "The Aristocracy of Culture." *Media, Culture and Society* 2, 3: 225–54.
——. (1984) *Distinction: A Social Critique of the Judgement of Taste.* Cambridge, MA: Harvard University Press.
Brown, Les and Savannah Waring, eds. (1983) *Fast Forward: The New Television and American Society.* Kansas City: Andrews and McMeel.
Browne, Nick. (1984) "The Political Economy of the Television (Super)Text." *Quarterly Review of Film Studies* 9 (Summer): 174–82.
Brunsdon, Charlotte. (1981) "Crossroads: Notes on Soap Opera." *Screen* 22, 4: 32–37.
——. (1983) "Crossroads: Notes on Soap Opera." In *Regarding Television: Critical Approaches—An Anthology,* ed. E. Ann Kaplan. American Film Institute Monograph Series, vol. 2. Frederick, MD.: University Publications of America.
Brunsdon, Charlotte and David Morley. (1978) *Everyday Television: Nationwide.* London: British Film Institute.
Budd, Mike and Clay Steinman. (1989) "Television, Cultural Studies, and the 'Blind Spot' Debate in Critical Communications Research." In *Television*

Studies: Textual Analysis, ed. Gary Burns and Robert J. Thompson. New York: Praeger.

Butler, Matilda and William Paisley. (1980) *Women and the Mass Media: Sourcebook for Research and Action.* New York: Human Sciences Press.

Byars, Jackie Louise. (1983) "Gender Representation in American Family Melodramas of the Nineteen-Fifties." Ph.D. diss., University of Texas at Austin.

——. (1987) "Reading Feminine Discourse: Prime-Time Television in the U.S." *Communication* 9: 289–303.

——. (1988) "Gazes/Voices/Power: Expanding Psychoanalysis for Feminist Film and Television Theory." In *Female Spectators: Looking at Film and Television*, ed. E. Deidre Pribram. New York: Verso.

Cantor, Muriel G. (1982) "Audience Control." In *Television: The Critical View*, ed. Horace Newcomb. New York: Oxford University Press.

Carter, Bill. (1991a) "Reporter's Notebook: Despite the Praise, These Shows Won't Be Back." *New York Times*, July 23, p. C13.

——. (1991b) "The Media Business: For Networks, Is No. 1 a Winner?" *New York Times*, Sept. 16, p. D1.

Chodorow, Nancy. (1978) *The Reproduction of Mothering: Psychoanalysis and the Sociology of Gender.* Berkeley: University of California Press.

Connell, Robert. W. (1987) *Gender and Power: Society, the Person and Sexual Politics.* Stanford, CA: Stanford University Press.

Conti, Delia. (1990) "The Rhetorical Battle Between the Stay-at-Home Mother and the Working Mother." Paper presented at the Northeast Popular Culture Association, Oct. 5–6.

Courtney, Alice E. and Thomas W. Whipple. (1980) *Sex Stereotyping in Advertising: An Annotated Bibliography.* Cambridge, MA: Marketing Science Institute.

Cowan, A. (1989) "Women's Gains on the Job: Not Without a Heavy Toll." *New York Times*, Aug. 21, pp. A1, A14.

Curran, James et al. (1982) "The Study of the Media: Theoretical Approaches." In *Culture, Society and the Media*, ed. Michael Gurevitch et al. New York: Methuen.

D'Acci, Julie. (1987) "The Case of Cagney and Lacey." In *Boxed In: Women and Television*, ed. Helen Baehr and Gillian Dyer. London: Pandora.

de Lauretis, Teresa. (1984) *Alice Doesn't: Feminism, Semiotics, Cinema.* Bloomington: Indiana University Press.

——. (1987) *Technologies of Gender: Essays on Theory, Film, and Fiction.* Bloomington: Indiana University Press.

Deleuze, Gilles and Felix Guattari. (1977) *Anti-Oedipus: Capitalism and Schizophrenia.* New York: Viking.

Deming, R. (1988) "Kate and Allie: New Women and the Audience's Television Archive." *Camera Obscura* 16: 15—66.

deMott, Benjamin. (1990) *The Imperial Middle: Why Americans Can't Think Straight About Class.* New York: William Morrow.

Doane, Mary Ann. (1987) *The Desire to Desire: The Woman's Film of the 1940's.* Bloomington: Indiana University Press.

Doane, Mary Ann et al. (1984) *Re-Vision: Essays in Feminist Film Criticism.* Frederick, MD: University Publications of America.

Drummond, Hugh. (1979) "Diagnosing Marriage." *Mother Jones* 4 (July).
Dusky, Lorraine. (1991) "Melanie Mayron's Sweet Success." *McCall's*, March, pp. 80–84, 150.
Dyer, Richard. (1981) "Entertainment and Utopia." In *"Genre, the Musical": A Reader*, ed. Rick Altman. London: Routledge and Kegan Paul.
Ehrenreich, Barbara. (1983) *The Hearts of Men: American Dreams and the Flight from Commitment.* Garden City, NY: Anchor Press/Doubleday.
——. (1989) *Fear of Falling: The Inner Life of the Middle Class.* New York: Pantheon.
Ehrenreich, Barbara and Frances Fox Piven. (1984) "The Feminization of Poverty." In *Alternatives: Proposals for America from the Democratic Left*, ed. Irving Howe. New York: Pantheon.
English, Deidre. (1983) "The Fear That Feminism Will Free Men First." In *Powers of Desire: The Politics of Sexuality*, ed. Ann Snitow et al. New York: Monthly Review Press.
Enzensberger, Hans Magnus. (1974) "Constituents of a Theory of the Media." In Enzensberger, *The Consciousness Industry: On Literature, Politics, and the Media.* New York: Seabury.
Epstein, Cynthia Fuchs. (1988) *Deceptive Distinctions: Sex, Gender and the Social Order.* New Haven, CT: Yale University Press.
Faludi, Susan. (1991) *Backlash: The Undeclared War Against American Women.* New York: Doubleday.
Feuer, Jane. (1984) "Melodrama, Serial Form and Television Today." *Screen* 25, 1: 4–16.
——. (1986) "Narrative Form in Television." In *High Theory, Low Culture: Analyzing Popular Television and Film*, ed. Colin MacCabe. Manchester: Manchester University Press.
Fiske, John. (1987) *Television Culture.* London: Methuen.
Flitterman-Lewis, Sandra. (1983) "The Real Soap Operas: TV Commercials." In *Regarding Television: Critical Approaches—An Anthology*, ed. E. Ann Kaplan. American Film Institute Monograph Series, vol. 2. Frederick, MD: University Publications of America.
——. (1987) "Psychoanalysis, Film, and Television." In *Channels of Discourse: Television and Contemporary Criticism*, ed. Robert C. Allen. Chapel Hill: University of North Carolina Press.
Fluck, Winifred. (1987) "Popular Culture as a Mode of Socialization." *Journal of Popular Culture* 21, 331: 31–46.
Foucault, Michel. (1973) *Madness and Civilization: A History of Insanity in the Age of Reason.* New York: Vintage.
——. (1975) *The Birth of the Clinic: An Archaeology of Medical Perception.* New York: Vintage.
——. (1979) *Discipline and Punish: The Birth of the Prison.* New York: Vintage/Random House.
——. (1980) *The History of Sexuality.* Volume 1: *An Introduction.* New York: Vintage/Random House.
——. (1984) *The Foucault Reader.* New York: Pantheon Books.
Franco, Jean. (1986) "The Incorporation of Women: A Comparison of North American and Mexican Popular Narrative." In *Studies in Entertainment: Critical Approaches to Mass Culture*, ed. Tania Modleski. Bloomington: Indiana University Press.

Friedan, Betty. (1963) *The Feminine Mystique.* New York: Norton.
——. (1986) *The Second Stage.* New York: Summit Books.
Gallagher, Margaret. (1981) *Unequal Opportunities: The Case of Women and the Media.* Paris: Unesco Press.
Galperin, William. (1988) "Sliding Off the Stereotype: Gender Difference in the Future of Television." In *Postmodernism and Its Discontents: Theories, Practices,* ed. E. Ann Kaplan. London: Verso.
Gerard, Jeremy. (1988) "TV Mirrors a New Generation." *New York Times,* Sunday, Oct. 30, Arts and Leisure Section 2, p. 28.
Gerbner, George. (1978) "The Dynamics of Cultural Resistance." In *Hearth and Home: Images of Women in the Mass Media,* ed. Gaye Tuchman et al. New York: Oxford University Press.
Gerson, Kathleen. (1985) *Hard Choices: How Women Decide About Work, Career, and Motherhood.* Berkeley: University of California Press.
Gerstel, Naomi and Harriet Engel Gross. (1987) *Families and Work: Towards Reconceptualization.* Philadelphia: Temple University Press.
Gilligan, Carol. (1982) *In a Different Voice: Psychological Theory and Women's Development.* Cambridge, MA: Harvard University Press.
Gitlin, Todd. (1978) "Media Sociology: The Dominant Paradigm." *Theory and Society* 6: 205–53.
——. (1985). *Inside Prime-Time.* New York: Pantheon.
——. (1986) *Watching Television.* Berkeley: University of California Press.
——. (1987) "Television's Screens: Hegemony in Transition." In *American Media and Mass Culture: Left Perspectives,* ed. Donald Lazere. Berkeley: University of California Press.
Gledhill, Christine. (1987) *Home Is Where the Heart Is: Studies in Melodrama and the Woman's Film.* London: British Film Institute.
Goodman, Ellen. (1990) "Where Were the Men in the Wellesley Flap?" *Pittsburgh Post-Gazette,* June 4, p. A7.
Gordon, Jill. (1991) "Mr. Right." In *Thirtysomething Stories,* ed. Edward Zwick and Marshall Herskovitz. New York: Pocket Books.
Gramsci, Antonio. (1972) *Selections from the Prison Notebooks of Antonio Gramsci.* New York: International Publishers.
Greer, Germaine. (1970) *The Female Eunuch.* London: MacGibbon and Kee.
Grossberg, Lawrence. (1983) "Cultural Studies Revisited and Revised." In *Communication in Transition: Issues and Debates in Current Research,* ed. Mary S. Mander. New York: Praeger.
Gurevitch, Michael et al., eds. (1982) *Culture, Society and the Media.* New York: Methuen.
Hacker, Andrew. (1986) "Women at Work." *New York Review* (Aug. 14).
Hall, Stuart. (1979) "Culture, the Media and the Ideological Effect." In *Mass Communication and Society,* ed. James Curran et al. Beverly Hills, CA: Sage.
——. (1981) "Encoding and Decoding in Television Discourse," In *Culture, Media, Language,* ed. Hall. London: Hutchinson.
——. (1982) "The Rediscovery of 'Ideology': Return of the Repressed in Media Studies." In *Culture, Society and the Media,* ed. Michael Gurevitch et al. New York: Methuen.
——. (1986) "On Postmodernism and Articulation: An interview with Stuart Hall." *Journal of Communication Inquiry* 10, 2: 45–60.
Hanke, Robert. (1990) "Hegemonic Masculinity in 'thirtysomething.'" *Critical*

Studies in Mass Communication 7: 231–48.

Hartmann, Heidi. (1980) "The Family as the Locus of Gender, Class and Political Struggle: The Example of Housework." *Signs* 6.

——. (1987) "Changes in Women's Economic and Family Roles in Post-World War II United States." In *Women, Households, and the Economy*, ed. Lourdes Beneria and Catherine R. Stimpson. New Brunswick, NJ: Rutgers University Press.

Haskell, Molly. (1987) *From Reverence to Rape.* Chicago: University of Chicago Press.

Hebdige, Dick. (1979) *Subculture: The Meaning of Style.* London and New York: Methuen.

Held, David. (1980) *Introduction to Critical Theory: Horkheimer to Habermas.* Berkeley: University of California Press.

Henkin, Josh. (1989) "Individualism Unbound: Reconsidering Modern-Day Romance." *Tikkun*; reprinted in *Utne Reader* (March/April).

Herman, Hank. (1988) "thirtysomething's Mel Harris: 'Prince Charming Lives'." *Health* (March).

Hersch, Patricia. (1988) "Thirtysomethingtherapy." *Psychology Today* (October): 62–63.

Hewlett, Sylvia. (1986) *A Lesser Life: The Myth of Women's Liberation in America.* New York: William Morrow.

Hirsch, Paul. (1982) "The Role of Television in Popular Culture." In *Television: The Critical View*, ed. Horace Newcomb. New York: Oxford University Press.

Hirshey, Gerri. (1989) "Coupledom Uber Alles: Tyranny of the Couples." *Washington Post Magazine;* reprinted in *Utne Reader* (March/April).

Hoban, Phoebe. (1988) "All in the Family" *New York Magazine* 29 (Feb. 29): 48 (5).

Hochschild, Arlie. (1989) *The Second Shift: Working Parents and the Revolution at Home.* New York: Viking.

Hoffman, Alice. (1988) "Move Over Ozzie and Harriet: Once TV Only Showed Typical Happy Families. A Crop of New Series Offers Everything But." *New York Times*, Feb. 14, Section 2, p. H1.

Huyssen, Andreas. (1986) "Mass Culture as Woman: Modernism's Other." In *Studies in Entertainment: Critical Approaches to Mass Culture*, ed. Tania Modleski. Bloomington: Indiana University Press.

Hymes, Dell H. (1972) "On Communicative Competence." In *Sociolinguistics*, ed. J. B. Pride and J. Holmes. Harmondsworth: Penguin.

Irigaray, Luce. (1980) "Ce sexe qui n'en est pas un". In *New French Feminisms,: An Anthology* ed. Elaine Marks and Isabelle de Courtivron. Amherst, MA: University of Massachusetts Press.

Jackman, Mary R. and Robert W. Jackman. (1983) *Class Awareness in the United States.* Berkeley: University of California Press.

Jameson, Fredric. (1979) "Reificiation and Utopia in Mass Culture." *Social Text* 1: 130–48.

——. (1983) "Postmodernism and the Consumer Society." In *Postmodern Culture*, ed. N. Foster. Seattle: Bay View.

Jay, Martin. (1973) *The Dialectical Imagination.* Boston: Little Brown.

Jensen, Julie. (1984) "An Interpretive Approach to Culture Production." In *Interpreting Television: Current Research Perspectives*, ed. Willard D. Rowland, Jr. and Bruce Watkins. Beverly Hills, CA: Sage.

Jhally, Sut and Justin Lewis. (1992) *Enlightened Racism: The Cosby Show, Audiences, and the Myth of the American Dream.* Boulder, CO: Westview.

Joyrich, Lynn. (1988) "All That Television Allows: TV Melodrama, Postmodernism and Consumer Culture." *Camera Obscura* 16: 129–53.

Kaplan, Cora. (1986). "The *Thorn Birds*": Fiction, Fantasy, Femininity." In *Formations of Fantasy,* ed. L. Burgin et al. New York: Methuen.

Kaplan, E. Ann. (1983) *Women and Film: Both Sides of the Camera.* New York: Methuen.

——. (1987) "Feminist Criticism and Television." In *Channels of Discourse: Television and Contemporary Criticism,* ed. Robert C. Allen. Chapel Hill: University of North Carolina Press.

——, ed. (1983) *Regarding Television: Critical Approaches—An Anthology.* American Film Institute Monograph Series, vol. 2. Frederick, MD: University Publications of America.

Katz, Elihu and Paul F. Lazarsfeld. (1955) *Personal Influence: The Part Played by People in the Flow of Mass Communications.* Glencoe, IL: Free Press.

Kellner, Douglas. (1987) "Re-Watching Television: Notes Towards a Political Criticism." *Diacritics* (Summer): 97–113.

——. (1992) "Popular Culture and the Construction of Postmodern Identities." In *Modernity and Identity,* ed. S. Lash and J. Friedman. Oxford: Basil Blackwell.

Kessler-Harris, Alice. (1982) *Out to Work: A History of Wage-Earning Women in the U.S.* New York: Oxford University Press.

Kristeva, Julia. (1980) *Desire in Language: A Semiotic Approach to Literature and Art,* ed. L. S. Roudiez. Oxford: Basil Blackwell.

Kroker, Arthur and David Cook. (1986) *The Postmodern Scene.* New York: St. Martin's Press.

Kuhn, Annette. (1982) *Women's Pictures: Feminism and Cinema.* London: Routledge and Kegan Paul.

——. (1985) *The Power of the Image: Essays on Representation and Sexuality.* London: Routledge and Kegan Paul.

Lacan, Jacques. (1977) *Ecrits: A Selection.* New York: Norton.

Langston, Donna. (1988) "Women and Work: Two Jobs for Less Than the Price of One." In *Changing Our Power: An Introduction to Women's Studies,* ed. J. Cochran. IA: Kendall/Hunt.

Lantos, Jeffrey. (1987) "Talking 'Bout My Generation." *American Film* 13, 2 (Nov. 23): 48.

Lasch, Christopher. (1977) *Haven in a Heartless World: The Family Besieged.* New York: Basic Books.

——. (1978) *The Culture of Narcissism.* New York: Norton.

Lazarre, Donald, ed. (1987) *American Media and Mass Culture: Left Perspectives.* Berkeley: University of California Press.

Lazarsfeld, Paul et al. (1948) *The People's Choice.* New York: Columbia University Press.

Lemon, Jackie. (1978) "Dominant or Dominated?" Women on Prime-Time Television." In *Hearth and Home: Images of Women in the Mass Media,* ed. Gaye Tuchman et al. New York: Oxford University Press.

Liebes, Tamar and Elihu Katz. (1990) *The Export of Meaning.* Oxford: Oxford University Press.

Loeb, Jane. (1990) "Rhetorical and Ideological Conservatism in thirtysomething." *Critical Studies in Mass Communication* 7: 249–60.

Long, Elizabeth. (1986) "Women, Reading, and Cultural Authority: Some Implications of the Audience Perspective in Cultural Studies." *American Quarterly* 38: 591–612.

——. (1989) "Feminism and Cultural Studies: Britain and America." *Critical Studies in Mass Communication* 6: 427–35.

Lowe, Carl, ed. (1981) *Television and American Culture.* New York: H. W. Wilson.

McRobbie, Angela. (1980) "Settling Accounts with Subculture: A Feminist Critique." *Screen Education* 34.

——. (1982a) "Jackie: An Ideology of Adolescent Femininity." In *Popular Culture, Past and Present: A Reader,* ed. B. Waites et al. London: Croom Helm.

——. (1982b) "The Politics of Feminist Research: Between Talk, Text and Action." *Feminist Review* 12: 46–57.

——. (1984) "Dance and Social Fantasy." In *Gender and Generation,* ed. McRobbie and Mica Nava. London: Macmillan.

Meehan, Diana. (1983) *Ladies of the Evening: Women Characters of Prime-Time Television.* Metuchen, NJ: Scarecrow.

Mellencamp, Patricia. (1986) "Situation Comedy, Feminism, and Freud: Discourses of Gracie and Lucy." In *Studies in Entertainment: Critical Approaches to Mass Culture,* ed. Tania Modleski. Bloomington: Indiana University Press.

Metz, Christian. (1982) *The Imaginary Signifier: Psychoanalysis and the Cinema.* Bloomington: Indiana University Press.

Meyrowitz, Joshua. (1985) *No Sense of Place: The Impact of Electronic Media on Social Behavior.* New York: Oxford University Press.

Miller, Mark Crispin. (1988) *Boxed In: The Culture of TV.* Evanston, IL: Northwestern University Press.

Millett, Kate. (1971) *Sexual Politics.* New York: Avon.

Minsky, Terry. (1990) "The Unbearable Heaviness of Being." *Esquire,* November. pp. 160–64.

Modleski, Tania. (1982) *Loving with a Vengeance: Mass Produced Fantasies for Women.* New York: Archon.

——, ed. (1986) *Studies in Entertainment: Critical Approaches to Mass Culture.* Bloomington: Indiana University Press.

Moffitt, Mary Ann. (1993) "Articulating Meaning: Reconceptions of the Meaning Process, Fantasy/Reality, and Identity in Leisure Activities." *Communication Theory* 3, 3 (August): 231–51.

Morley, David (1986) *Family Television: Cultural Power and Domestic Leisure.* London: Comedia.

——. (1989) "Changing Paradigms in Audience Studies." In *Remote Control: Television, Audiences, and Cultural Power.,* ed. Ellen Seiter et al. London and New York: Routledge.

——. (1993) "Active Audience Theory: Pendulums and Pitfalls." *Journal of Communication* 43, 4: 13–20.

"Motherhood Is Even Sweeter the Second Time Around!" (1991) *Redbook,* May, pp. 26-28.

Mulvey, Laura. (1975) "Visual Pleasure and Narrative Cinema." *Screen* 16, 3 (Autumn): 6–18.

Nelson, Cary and Lawrence Grossberg, eds. (1988) *Marxism and the Interpretation of Culture.* Champaign: University of Illinois Press.

Newcomb, Horace and Paul M. Hirsch. (1984) "Television as a Cultural Forum:

Implications for Research." In *Interpreting Television: Current Research Perspectives,* ed. Willard D. Rowland, Jr. and Bruce Watkins. Beverly Hills, CA: Sage.

O'Connor, John. (1989) "The Series for These Ambiguous Times." *New York Times,* May 30, p. C20.

——. (1990) The Jewish Hero Comes of Age." *New York Times,* Arts and Leisure Sec. July 15, pp. 25, 30.

——. (1991) "A Stylish Throwback with a Modern Twist." *New York Times,* April 16, Arts and Leisure Section, p. C11.

Oakley, Ann. (1974) *The Sociology of Housework.* New York: Vintage.

Parkin, Frank. (1979) *Marxism and Class Theory: A Bourgeois Critique.* New York: Columbia University Press.

Parsons, Talcott and Robert F. Bales. (1955) *Family Socialization and Interaction Process.* New York: Free Press.

"Patty Wettig and Ken Olin: Love and Trust—That's What Marriage is All About." (1991) *Redbook,* February, p. 26.

Pleck, Joseph. (1977) "The Work-Family Role System." *Social Problems* 24 (April): 417–27.

Press, Andrea. (1987) "Deconstructing the Female Audience: Class Differences in Women's Identification with Television Narrative and Characters." Ph.D. diss., University of California, Berkeley.

——. (1990) "Class, Gender and the Female Viewer: Women's Responses to 'Dynasty'." In *Television and Women's Culture: The Politics of the Popular,* ed. Mary Ellen Brown. London: Sage.

——. (1991) *Women Watching Television: Gender, Class, and Generation in the American Television Experience.* Philadelphia: University of Pennsylvania Press.

Press kit from *thirtysomething,* 2nd season. (1988) Culver City, CA: Bedford Falls Productions.

Pribram, E. Deidre, ed. (1988) *Female Spectators: Looking at Film and Television.* London: Verso.

Radway, Janice. (1987) *Reading the Romance: Women, Patriarchy and Popular Literature.* London: Verso.

Rapping, Elaine. (1986) "Hollywood's New "Feminist" Heroines." *Cineaste* 14, 4: 4–9.

Robertson, Ian. (1987) *Sociology.* New York: Worth.

Robinson, Lillian. (1978) "What's My Line? Telefiction and Women's Work." In Robinson, *Sex, Class and Culture.* Bloomington: Indiana University Press.

Rosen, Jay. (1989) "Thirtysomething." *Tikkun* 4, 4 (July/August).

Rosen, Marjorie. (1973) *Popcorn Venus: Women, Movies, and the American Dream.* New York: Coward, McCann and Geoghegan.

Rowland, Willard D., Jr. and Bruce Watkins, eds. (1984) *Interpreting Television: Current Research Perspectives.* Beverly Hills, CA: Sage.

Rubin, Lillian B. (1976) *Worlds of Pain: Life in the Working-Class Family.* New York: Basic Books.

——. (1990) *Women of a Certain Age: The Midife Search for Self.* New York: Harper and Row.

Ruddick, Sara. (1982) "Maternal Thinking." In Ruddick, *Rethinking the Family: Some Feminist Questions.* New York: Longman.

Ryan, Mary. (1979) "Femininity and Capitalism in Antebellum America." In *Capitalist Patriarchy and the Case for Socialist Feminism,* ed. Z. R. Eisenstein. New

York: Monthly Review Press.

Schwichtenberg, Cathy. (1989) "Feminist Cultural Studies." *Critical Studies in Mass Communication* (June): 202–7.

Seiter, Ellen. (1987) "Semiotics and Television." In *Channels of Discourse: Television and Contemporary Criticism,* ed. Robert C. Allen. Chapel Hill: University of North Carolina Press.

Seiter, Ellen, Hans Borcher, G. Kreutzner, and E. M. Warth, eds. (1989) *Remote Control: Television Audiences and Cultural Power.* London: Routledge.

Shilliday, Susan. (1991) "Therapy." In *Thirtysomething Stories,* ed. Edward Zwick and Marshall Herskovitz. New York: Pocket Books.

Silverman, Kaja. (1983) *The Subject of Semiotics.* New York: Oxford University Press.

——. (1988) *The Acoustic Mirror: The Female Voice in Psychoanalysis and Cinema.* Bloomington: Indiana University Press.

Stacey, J. (1986) "Are Feminists Afraid to Leave Home? The Challenge of Conservative Pro-Family Feminism." In *What Is Feminism: A Re-Examination,* ed. Juliet Mitchell and Ann Oakley. New York: Pantheon.

Stack, Carol. (1974) *All Our Kin: Strategies for Survival in a Black Community.* New York: Harper and Row.

Steeves, H. Leslie. (1987) "Feminist Theories and Media Studies." *Media Studies in Mass Communications* 4, 2: 95–135.

Streeter, Thomas. (1984) "An Alternative Approach to Television Research: Developments in British Cultural Studies at Birmingham." In *Interpreting Television: Current Research Perspectives,* ed Willard D. Rowland, Jr. and Bruce Watkins. Beverly Hills, CA: Sage.

Taylor, Ella. (1988) "Forget Murder and Car Chases: Now It's "Slice of Life" Shows." *New York Times,* April 17, Section 2, p. H39.

——. (1989) *Prime-Time Families: Television Culture in Post-War America.* Berkeley: University of California Press.

"Thirtysomething": A Chronicle of Everyday Life." (1988) *New York Times,* February 24, p. C26.

Tilly, Louise and Joan Scott. (1978) *Women, Work, and Family.* New York: Holt, Rinehart and Winston.

Torres, Sasha. (1989) "Melodrama, Masculinity and the Family: Thirtysomething as Therapy." *Camera Obscura* 19: 87–106.

Tuchman, Gaye. (1978) "The Symbolic Annihilation of Women by the Mass Media." In *Hearth and Home: Images of Women in the Mass Media,* ed. Tuchman et al. New York: Oxford University Press.

Tulloch, John. (1990) *Television Drama: Agency, Audience and Myth.* London: Routledge.

Wallis, Claudia. (1989) "Onward Women!" *Time* , December 4.

Watt, Ian. (1957) *The Rise of the Novel.* Harmondsworth: Penguin.

"Why We're *Still* Watching and Arguing About 'thirtysomething.'" (1990). *Entertainment Weekly,* May 4.

Williams, Linda. (1988) "Feminist Film Theory: Mildred Pierce and the Second World War." In *Female Spectators: Looking at Film and Television,* ed. E. Deidre Pribram, New York: Verso.

Williams, Raymond (1977) "A Lecture on Realism." *Screen* 18: 1.

Zwick, Edward and Marshall Herskovitz, eds. (1991) *Thirtysomething Stories.* New York: Pocket Books.

Index

This book was set in Baskerville and Eras typefaces. Baskerville was designed by John Baskerville at his private press in Birmingham, England, in the eithteenth century. The first typeface to depart from the oldstyle typeface design, Baskerville has more variation between thick and thin strokes. In an effort to ensure that the thick end thin strokes of his typeface reproduced well on paper, John Baskerville developed the first wove paper, the surface of which was much smoother than the laid paper of the time. The development of wove paper was partly responsible for the introduction of typefaces classifiied as modern, which have even more contrast between thick and thin strokes.

Eras was designed in 1969 by Studio Hollenstein in Paris for the Wagner Typefoundry. A contemporary script-like sans-serif typeface, the letters of Eras have a monotone stroke and are slightly inclined.

Printed on acid-free paper.